MARY OF NAZARETH
SIGN AND INSTRUMENT OF CHRISTIAN UNITY

MARY OF NAZARETH
SIGN AND INSTRUMENT OF CHRISTIAN UNITY

*A Biblical Exposition of Mary and
Her Relation to the Problem of Christian Unity*

by
Kenneth J. Howell

Queenship

PUBLISHING COMPANY
P.O. Box 220, Goleta, CA 93116
(800) 647-9882 • (805) 692-0043 • Fax: (805) 967-5843

Library of Congress Number # 97-076236

Published by:
    Queenship Publishing
    P.O. Box 220
    Goleta, CA 93116
    (800) 647-9882 • (805) 692-0043 • Fax: (805) 967-5843

Printed in the United States of America

ISBN: 1-57918-061-2

TABLE OF CONTENTS

PREFACE

Mary is not a subject I would naturally choose to write about. At my confirmation in the Roman Catholic Church on 1 June 1996, I affirmed everything that "This holy Catholic Church teaches" and so my beliefs contained a complete assent to all that the Church teaches about Mary. But Mary remained doctrines to be believed, not a person to be loved and cherished. The mother of Jesus was largely absent from the first forty-four years of my life. Besides the occasional sermon on Mary around Christmas, I spent very little time thinking about Jesus' mother during the eighteen years of my Presbyterian ministry and teaching.

Soon after my reception into the Catholic Church, I realized that I needed to grow in my relationship with Mary, and so I began praying for a deeper knowledge of and devotion to the mother of Jesus. In essence I said to Jesus, "Help me to love your mother as you do." It also bothered me that I could grasp and defend each of the major Marian doctrines, but I had little understanding of how they fit together, mutually implying one another.

Over the course of the next year, I experienced what seemed like yet another conversion. By Christmas the thoughts of my heart had a distinctly Marian tinge. My love for Jesus' mother was growing as I prayed for understanding of Mary's role in her Son's life. In January of 1997, I asked a small group of Catholic theologians to explain to me how all the Catholic doctrines about Mary fit together. They assured me that such understanding would come in time. Little did I realize how quickly my prayer would be answered. The understanding I desired began to grow by June of 1997 when I became convinced from a deepening life of prayer that I should write about Mary and the problem of Christian unity.

The book you are about to read seeks to explain from the Scriptures some of the treasures about Mary which have become integral to my spiritual life. Although I am an academic by training, this book is not an academic treatise. I have chosen to forego the usual scholarly apparati such as footnotes and digressions in favor of a spiritual meditation. The perceptive reader will see that my writing grows out of scholarly engagement with the texts of the Bible, but reading this book as an academic explanation will surely miss its purpose. As the book grew out of prayer, it must be read in the same spirit.

There are many people whose lives and time are hidden investments in this book. Among the many priests who have ministered to me, several have led me to ever deeper understandings of the Catholic faith and of Mary. Fr. Francis Cosgrove spent countless hours with me as I journeyed to the Catholic Church. Fr. Paul Vota M.J. has shown an enormous trust in me as a Christian and as a Catholic speaker. I owe much to the Miles Jesu family. Fr. Luke Laslavich O.Praem. guided me to and through the final stages of my own Marian consecration. Among Catholic theologians and thinkers from whom I have profited I must mention Professors Scott Hahn, John Saward and especially Mark Miravalle. I am privileged to have been treated with such kindness by a Marian scholar of Dr. Miravalle's stature. Several friends helped immensely in commenting on the manuscript version of this work: Sheila Beingessner, Barbara Brown, Scott Butler, Lynn Nordhagen, Fr. Luke Laslavich. I especially want to thank Marcus Grodi, the director of the *Coming Home Network International*. Mr. Grodi's friendship and support have been one of the most important of my life. Also, Lucille Cortese and the staff of St. Joseph Radio have been a constant encouragement to finish this project. Thanks too to my special friends in the Bloomington Catholic community who undergirded this ministry in prayer. Finally, I want to thank my father and mother, Kevin and Mary Howell as well as my wife Sharon, who though not Catholic, have been my constant supporters in life and in ministry.

Kenneth J. Howell Ph.D.
25 March 1998 — Feast of the Annunciation

INTRODUCTION

MARY AND THE PROBLEM OF
CHRISTIAN UNITY

We are living in a remarkable age. As we approach the third millennium of Christianity in the year 2,000, we are watching a world in extremes. Amid the rapid onslaught of secularization and irreligion, we find hordes of people seeking solace in religion. Amid the ravages of war and violence, we find the comfort and love of those who care for the poor and disadvantaged. Amid the lightening pace of modern life, we find souls searching for deeper meaning by retreating to monasteries and ashrams for solitude.

Two of the most powerful inspirations in late twentieth century Christianity are the drive toward greater unity among Christians of widely differing backgrounds (ecumenism) *and* the rapid growth of Marian devotion all around the world. This century has seen unprecedented efforts to bring together Christians who have been separated by misunderstanding and prejudice. And just when the ecumenical movement on a formal level seemed moribund, a new surge of grassroots ecumenism is finding ways of bringing together Catholic, Orthodox and Protestant Christians. No matter what the outcome of these efforts may be, the air of this last decade of the second millennium is filled with the scent of Christian unity. It seems that Christians are grasping every opportunity to reconcile their doctrinal differences and to find the sweet savor of "brothers dwelling together in unity" (Ps 133: 1).

If this is an age of ecumenism, it is equally a Marian era because no century since the birth of Christ has witnessed such an outpouring of devotion to the mother of Jesus. As many observers note, reported apparitions and locutions have multiplied, leading numerous Christians to an unprecedented devotion to the humble handmaiden of the Lord who was privileged to bring the world its Redeemer. In tandem with these grassroots movements, there is a monumental effort within the Catholic Church for the Pope to define as dogma Marian doctrines that have long been present in the Church (Mediatrix, Coredemptrix, Advocate). Whether the Supreme Pontiff of the Catholic Church decides to act, there is likely to be no diminishing of devotion to the mother of Jesus.

On the other hand, many non-Catholic Christians are mystified by such devotion to Mary. Some feel strangely drawn to honor her, but are afraid of falling into excessive focus on Mary to the exclusion of Jesus. To others, Marian devotion borders on the blasphemous. To still others, Catholics are idolaters. It is not an overstatement to say that no expression of historic Christianity has ever placed Mary in such a high position of honor as has the western Catholic tradition. And even though the Eastern Orthodox Churches have long honored Mary as the Mother of God, they do not have fully developed mariologies as the Western Church has.

The juxtaposition of ecumenical and Marian movements seems odd at best. On the surface, it appears that Mary would be the last subject chosen in an ecumenical dialogue. One might think that all the areas on which common agreement might be achieved should be addressed first, and then deal with the thorny question of Marian doctrine. Better to leave Mary until last. However, I am now convinced that questions about Mary must be addressed up front if any true ecumenism is ever to be achieved. On a purely human level, no genuine friendship can ignore beliefs which are central to one party while those same beliefs are at best questionable to the other. Further, it is not completely honest for Catholics to pretend that Marian doctrines and devotions are not important and central to our lives. We ought to state openly that the Catholic faith does not allow the Church to ever change its defined dogmas about Mary. On the other hand, we must admit that not everything that goes on under the term Marian devotion is necessary or beneficial for the Church.

Purpose and Themes

What can talk about Mary do to promote the cause of ecumenism? The answer depends on what we mean by *ecumenism.* One definition — and the one most common — sees ecumenism as a process of negotiation between different churches whereby one church gives up some aspect of its faith and the other partner relinquishes its claim to some of its distinctives. This process proceeds through a number of steps until a lowest common denominator is reached. The result is a church or some other official body which has a reduced form of faith and practice so that it might accommodate each respective member. This has largely been the pattern of ecumenism in the United States and the Western world for the better part of this century. In my judgment, such attempts have been a monumental failure. Mary cannot help with this type of ecumenism.

The other definition of ecumenism is not founded on the concept of negotiation, but on seeking together the truth of God's revelation. It begins with confessing that we don't apprehend God's truth completely, and that we must always seek to have the mind of Christ. In this conception, unity of heart and mind does not come from negotiated agreements, but from all parties recognizing and embracing the objective truth of God. It is a commonplace that married couples do not achieve success by each giving fifty percent to their marriage, but by each giving one hundred percent of themselves. In the same way, Christian unity comes from full commitment to searching for truth in a spirit of humility. Ecumenism begins with recognizing that unity already exists in God, that Christ is the center of unity, and that the Holy Spirit is the operative agent in bringing Christians together. Mary has everything to do with this kind of ecumenism.

The purpose of this book is to show that by knowing Mary better, we come to know Jesus Christ her Son better. Jesus Christ is the only source of our salvation and Christian unity. When we realize that the unity of the church already exists in Jesus Christ, it is more likely that we will come humbly and obediently to Him as the source of truth and unity. Yet many have said that Christ is the source of unity, but there are still numerous and conflicting views of what that means in practice. How can we be open and honest about our common love for Christ and still have a common path to unity?

I contend in this book that Jesus Christ is an inexhaustible wellspring of grace such that we can never plumb the depths of his truth and love. I am convinced that Christians are not unified because we fail to understand fully who Christ is. And that is why Mary is so important. The only Christ who redeems us from sin is the one born of the Virgin Mary. To have the right Jesus, we must know who Mary is. We must follow Jesus as he came to us through Mary. It was this same essential truth that was recognized centuries ago at the Council of Ephesus (A.D. 431) when the Fathers of the Church declared Mary the Mother of God. Their statement recognized that we can only call Jesus Christ God if Mary is called the Mother of God. What came from her womb that night in Bethlehem was not just a man, nor a god, but the perfect God-Man.

I invite the reader to join me as we explore how knowing Mary better can deepen our knowledge of Jesus Christ her Son. I offer to the reader the opportunity to look again more closely at the New Testament to see what we can learn about the source and power of our unity as Christians. I ask the reader to come back in time — from Bethlehem to Calvary — to follow the lives of Jesus and Mary through joy and suffering so that we might emerge in the future as a whole and healed people. God wants to heal our divisions, but we must allow his scalpel to perform its divine surgery.

How to Read this Book

Books can be read in different ways and this book must be read in a certain way to understand it properly. I encourage the reader to have a Bible beside him as he reads, looking up references and relating them to the point being made. This is especially true of those texts in the Bible that I spend a good amount of time explaining. My explanations will not mean much until the reader is familiar with the biblical text. All the biblical texts quoted in this book are my own translations from the original languages of Scripture. At times, they are close to some of the standard translations; at others, I translate in a way that highlights a particular aspect of the text.

The reader also will understand my points better if he places himself inside the biblical stories with the use of his imagination. As a teacher of Sacred Scripture for many years, I often saw that my students' lack of ability to understand the Bible came more from lack of imagination than from not knowing the words. A third feature is meditating on the certain key biblical words (e.g. *kecharitomene* in Lk 1:28). Marian texts in the Bible require an in-depth searching of key words and phrases that unlock new worlds, worlds that were closed to me for many years.

Understanding this book requires knowing how the chapters fit together into the whole. Since my theme is how Mary is a sign and instrument of Christian unity, **Chapters One and Two** introduce us to the person and life of Mary. Mary's character shines through the world of sin and selfishness to reveal a young woman totally devoted to God. Mary's faith allows her to cooperate with her Son's unique salvation in bringing all the children of God to glory.

Chapter Three poses the problem of Christian unity in terms of some ways in which various ecumenical efforts have pursued that goal without success. I try to show that some of those ways are fatally flawed. I also show from John chapter seventeen and Ephesians chapter four that those failed attempts at unity have missed an essential ingredient, the objective unity that already exists in God.

Chapter Four outlines the divine plan of salvation in a way that shows how essential Mary's role is. I am convinced that much of the New Testament is misunderstood by contemporary Christians because they do not understand the plan of salvation that God had been preparing for his people in the Old Testament. Ironically, those who call themselves New Testament Christians often misunderstand the New Testament because they have ignored the Old. I show *the patterns of salvation history* that come to fulfillment in the Messiah. Those patterns are not only fulfilled by the Messiah but by the mother who gave him birth.

Chapter Five explains how Jesus Christ alone is the Savior of our fallen human race. The unique person and work of Jesus Christ is predicted and assumed by the Old Testament and is explained much more fully by the New Testament writers. In keeping with this biblical pattern, the Catholic Church teaches us that "there is no other name given under heaven by which we can be saved" (Acts 4:12). The salvation Jesus came to give is full and rich, a salvation that Mary fully experienced and proclaimed. Embracing Mary as Jesus's mother requires understanding Jesus' unique role as our Redeemer.

Chapter Six explains the scriptural principle of human cooperation in God's plan of salvation. Christ is the world's only Savior but without men and women to carry out his salvation, the world would still be lost. Jesus Christ accomplished the work of salvation in this world, providing the unrepeatable foundation for our eternal happiness. Yet his saving work goes on through the application of his work to human hearts. He called men and women into his service to carry his salvation to the ends of the earth and to witness to it with their words and lives.

Chapter Seven develops the theme of Mary's role more fully by applying the principles of the previous chapters to Mary. Mary's importance in the biblical stories results from the unique relationship she bears to the Son of God who alone is the world's Redeemer. That relationship with Jesus allows Mary to participate in his saving work as our spiritual mother. As one who has been completed in grace, Mary functions as advocate and mediatrix for the people of God.

Chapter Eight applies the principles of the previous chapters to our current situation by showing more fully Mary's role in Christian unity. Jesus' mother leads us to the only One who can unify Christians, Jesus Christ.

I now invite you into Mary's world, the world of biblical truth where we can together find her Son, Jesus the Christ. And like the Magi of old, when we find Jesus, we will also find him with his mother (Mt 2:11).

CHAPTER ONE

MARY: A WOMAN FOR ALL CHRISTIANS

What kind of woman was Mary of Nazareth? As is true of Jesus, we know nothing of Mary's physical appearance or demeanor. But the historical sources give us a rather detailed picture of Mary's character. Several historical sources give us much biographical information about Mary and they may be fairly reliable documents, but in this book I want to ask what we can learn from the canonical Scriptures about Mary's life and character.

It's often heard that the Bible says very little about Mary, but a closer look at Scripture reveals something quite different. If we use even the most superficial of criteria (i.e. number of words and verses), the New Testament says more about Mary than it does on topics everyone considers essential. For example, the very important parallelism between Adam and Christ in Paul's epistles occupies only two passages with a total of thirteen verses (Rom 5:12-21 ten verses & I Cor. 15:21-23 three verses). Passages about Mary in the birth narrative of Luke's Gospel alone occupy eighty-two verses. And this isn't counting Matthew, Mark and John. My personal experience as a non-Catholic Christian convinced me that I couldn't find much about Mary because I wasn't looking for it. Also, the Scriptures sometimes teach deep and rich truths in a very short space. For example, the topic of justification by faith occupies a very small portion of the New Testament — it's only discussed directly in Romans, Galatians and James 2:14-26 — but it has played an enormously important role in the history of the Christian faith. Thus, it is unwise to conclude that the amount of verses devoted to a topic in the Bible is directly linked to its importance. In any case, there's more in the Bible about Mary than is often supposed.

The course of Mary's life follows that of Jesus' life, a fact that shows how her life was united with his throughout her earthly pilgrimage. We first meet Mary, of course, in the stories of Jesus' birth. God in his wisdom has chosen to give us the account of Jesus' birth in much greater detail than was necessary. And from two quite different vantage points. Only two of the four evangelists give us any detail regarding Jesus' conception, Matthew and Luke. Their accounts are very different but not in contradiction with one another. Matthew concentrates on Joseph and Luke on Mary but both accounts are detailed and intricate. In this chapter, we will look at Mary's life leading up to the birth and early life of her Son. In the next chapter, we will explore Mary's life in connection with Jesus' public ministry. Why did the Holy Spirit inspire the scriptural writers to say so much where less would do? Part of the reason has to do with Mary herself. Let's look at her life in the New Testament.

Gabriel Announces Jesus' Conception (Luke 1:26-38)

Luke gives us the events that happen first, beginning even before Mary finds out that she will give birth to God's Son. In the ancient world, the arrival of a king was preceded by a herald who was to announce the coming of the King. This is why Luke spends so much time telling us about the birth of John the Baptist. He is the one who will announce the arrival of the new king. Only in John's case, his birth is also remarkable, if not miraculous. This birth confirms the pattern of salvation of the Old Testament. God's saving action is accompanied by astounding births to emphasize that this salvation can only come from God. John the Baptist is born of a woman who was beyond the years of childbearing to prepare for an even more miraculous birth than his own, a birth from a virgin. John announces Jesus's arrival not only by his words but by his own birth. Both births cause wonder but the virgin birth stresses that what is impossible with human power is within God's power "because nothing will be impossible with God" (Lk 1:37).

Gabriel's greeting to Mary is very unusual. "Hail, full of grace one. The Lord is with you." (Lk 1:28). We will return to this greeting in more detail in Chapter Seven, but let's note here how Mary responds to Gabriel's greeting. Mary is immediately troubled and begins to reason out the meaning of the greeting. Beyond the obvious fact that any normal person would have been startled by the presence of an angel, Luke tells us the greeting itself troubled Mary (Lk 1:29). Why? Probably because he calls her "full of grace or highly favored." I will explain the full meaning of this word later. What does Mary's response tell us about her attitude? It shows Mary's humility in that she did not think herself worthy of this title. Mary was full of grace, as Gabriel said, but she was not aware of it. This is true of many people who have great humility. They are unaware of their virtue.

Mary asks all the normal human questions when Gabriel tells her that she will conceive the Son of God in her womb through the Holy Spirit (Lk 1:34). Yet I don't think that it was just the manner of the birth that was startling. It was also that the child within her would be God himself ("the Son of the most High"). For a normal Jewish woman of the first century nothing could have been more unbelievable. The Jews emphasized in their creed that God is sovereign Lord of all (Dt 6:4 "Hear, O Israel, the Lord our God is One"). This belief was reinforced in the story of the building of the first temple when Solomon prayed "But will God really dwell on earth? The heavens, the highest heavens cannot contain you. How much less this temple I have built!" (I Ki 8:27). And yet God did choose to place his presence in that temple as was shown through the descent of the pillar of cloud that came down (see I Ki 8:10-11). Mary could have legitimately reasoned, "The temple is one thing; my womb is another." Gabriel's words assure her that the Holy Spirit will overshadow her just as he once did the temple of God in Israel. In a very real sense, Mary becomes a tabernacle or temple where God dwells on earth. This is why she has been called *the Ark of the New Covenant* in the history of the Church. She was to the new covenant people of God what the Ark of the Covenant was to Israel. She brought the presence of God to the people of God.

The most remarkable part of Mary's response is her faith. Lk 1:38 reads, "Behold, the handmaid of the Lord. Let it be to me according to your word." The words "let it be" (*genoito*) are translated into Latin as *fiat*, a word that has passed into English to describe God's creation of the world when he said, "Let there be light etc." Mary's *fiat* is her YES to God and shows that she really is what Gabriel called her, full of grace. How could she say YES to God's will for her life unless she had been prepared by grace to respond so positively and so readily to God? There is more here than meets the eye. When Mary says, "let it be to me" she is giving her full consent to the will of God for her life. Imagine the shame she knew she would have to bear because of this event. Imagine her natural doubt and understandable questions. Yet her heart and soul were so detached from the world's praise or condemnation that she responded without any hesitancy by saying YES to God. Through her cooperation with God's plan of salvation, we have the Savior who rescues us from sin.

Mary's humility and faith are clear examples for us. Both virtues come from the same source, a heart that has been filled with grace. Humility in our lives will produce the same response that Mary had. It will make us also say that we are the Lord's servants and that we are ready to do his will. If we have Mary's faith, we will say YES to God when he asks of us the unusual and even the heroic. You and I can never duplicate Mary's role of bearing the Son of God, but we can respond with the same humble submission to the will of God as we are enabled by grace to do so. Luke tells us so much about Mary's faith because he wants us to see her as our example of faith and humility.

Mary Visits Elizabeth (Luke 1:39-56)

Almost immediately after Mary learned that she was to bear the Son of God, she hurried to visit her relative Elizabeth. Like the Annunciation, this event in Mary's life holds a deep meaning for those who meditate on its truth. Most Catholics are familiar with this story since it is the Second of the Joyful Mysteries that one meditates on in the Rosary. The Visitation unveils much about Mary for here is where we find her song of joy, her *Magnificat*. Understanding this famous song requires seeing the relationship between Elizabeth and Mary. Mary's natural reaction to Gabriel's news was to go to Elizabeth because she now understood that the birth of her Son, the Messiah, had a much wider significance than for her personally. When she was told that her relative Elizabeth, who had been called barren (Lk 1:36), was to give birth, Mary wanted to share in Elizabeth's joy. She also wanted to tell of her own pregnancy that Gabriel had announced. Luke tells us that Elizabeth was filled with the Holy Spirit (Lk 1:41), and spoke words of prophecy to Mary. Her first words were, "blessed are you among women and blessed is the fruit of your womb." (Lk 1:42). It would have been natural for Elizabeth to tell Mary of her own supernatural pregnancy. She had given up the hope of ever having her own child. The six months of her pregnancy before Mary came must have been a time of constant joy because there was nothing greater for Jewish women in the ancient world than to bear a child. Yet Elizabeth's words do not reflect the natural response of her own joy, but her happiness in now seeing the mother of the Lord come to her (Lk 1:43). Luke does not indicate that Mary told Elizabeth anything, only that she greeted her. It was the movement of John the Baptist in Elizabeth's womb that told her of the Holy One who was coming hidden in Mary's womb.

The fruit of Mary's womb is also blessed, says Elizabeth (Lk 1:42). This is true but for a very different reason than Mary's being blessed. Mary was blessed because God dwelt within her, but the fruit of her womb was God himself. When Elizabeth calls Mary's child blessed, it is more akin to the Psalmist who says, "Bless the Lord, O my soul. All that is within me bless his holy name." (Ps 103:1). When blessing is ascribed to a human being like Mary, it means that she is the recipient of divine favor and goodness. When blessing is ascribed to God, it is a recognition that God has blessedness in and of himself. He has not received that blessing from anyone but rather is the *source* of blessing for others. The fruit of Mary's womb is blessed because that child possesses all blessing and happiness within himself. He became the source of Mary's being blessed.

Elizabeth knew herself to be blessed as well because *the mother of God* had come to her. These few short words say volumes, *how is it then that the mother of my Lord would come to me?* (Lk 1:43). Elizabeth's sense of being blessed is balanced by her amazement at being visited by God himself. If we had been Elizabeth, we might have said, *how is it that God himself would come to me?* And our words would not have been inappropriate. Yet Elizabeth's actual words afford insight into a biblical view of Mary and her Son Jesus. These words suggest a theme resident in the Old Testament Scriptures. When God comes to earth, the ground he touches becomes holy (see Ex 3:5). So here, God comes in an unprecedented manner, in bodily fashion, and the ground on which he stands becomes holy too. Mary's womb becomes holy ground, a sacred dwelling of the Most High, because God's glory is too radiant and effervescent to be contained within the few decimeters of a Virgin's womb. Elizabeth honors Mary because God has honored Mary with his presence.

Why was Mary blessed? Because she was the physical bearer of God's Son? Yes, but more. It was because she believed what Gabriel told her. This is stressed in Luke 1:38 when she says YES to God's plan and in Luke 1:45 when Elizabeth recognizes Mary's implicit trust in God ("Blessed is she who believed that there would be a fulfillment of the things spoken by the Lord"). Mary's greatest blessing comes from her faith in God's plan of salvation, and she rejoiced just to be a part of it. And the same is true for each of us who follow Jesus. Paul speaks of himself as an instrument of reconciling the world to God in 2 Corinthians 5:16-21. Paul pleads for reconciliation "as if God were making his appeal through us." The ministry of reconciliation that Paul had was God's work through Paul. Mary and Paul become examples for each of us who are baptized into Christ. We become God's instruments of salvation for others when we give ourselves to God in faith as Mary did.

Mary's faith had to be expressed verbally, and the most natural way for a young Jewish woman was to break forth in song. But Mary's *Magnificat* — the name derives from the first word in the Latin translation — is more than an impromptu canticle. It is a song modelled on the pattern of the Old Testament Psalms that adore the true and living God for his redeeming love. In addition to the entire one hundred and fifty Psalms, Mary's song recalls the Songs of Moses (Ex 15:1-18) and of Deborah (Jud 5:1-31). Both these Old Testament hymns celebrate God's saving victory over his enemies. Yet the closest parallel is unquestionably Hannah's song of praise in 1 Samuel 2:1-10. Here are a few of the parallels:

The Opening Words of Praise

Hannah: My heart rejoices in the Lord
My horn exalts in the Lord...
For I rejoiced in Your salvation (1 Sam 2:1)

Mary: My soul magnifies the Lord
My spirit is glad in God my Savior (Lk 1:46)

The Character of God

Hannah: There is none holy like the Lord
There is none besides you
There is no rock like our God (1 Sam 2:2)

Mary: The Mighty One has done great things
Holy is His name
His mercy is forever and ever
On those who fear him (Lk 1:49,50)

The Reversal of Human Fortunes

Hannah: The Lord kills and gives life
He brings down to Sheol and lifts up
The Lord makes poor and makes rich
He degrades and he exalts
He raises the poor from the dust
He lifts the beggar from the ash heap (1 Sam 2:6,7)

Mary: He threw down the powerful from their thrones
And exalted the humble
He filled the hungry with good things
And sent the rich away empty. (Lk 1:52,53)

Hannah's and Mary's responses to God are controlled by the theme of God looking on the lowliness and humility of His servants. Their joy in God's saving power comes from their humble recognition of His sovereign choice of each of them as the divine instrument. Hannah knew that the boy given to her was destined to be a prophet. Mary knew that the boy given to her was destined to be the Messiah. We will see in Chapter Four how this theme of miraculous birth permeated the Old Testament just in order to prepare for Christ's birth. The songs of Mary and Hannah are not simply those of Jewish women wanting children. They express the joy of God's handmaidens in the salvation He brought to His people. Mary called God her Savior (Lk 1: 47) because she had completely identified herself with Israel as God's people, and therefore longed for the redemption of her people. But Mary's situation also differed from Hannah's too. Hannah carried within her womb a future prophet of Israel. Mary carried the Hope of Israel. Hanna's son would point to the future redemption. Mary's Son was the redemption. Hannah's pregnancy was an answer to her prayer. Mary's pregnancy was a complete surprise. Hannah lived in hope of the fulfillment; Mary lived the fulfillment.

Mary and Elizabeth perceived with a skill, with which women seem especially endowed, that their lives would be henceforth bound to God's saving plan. Any woman knows that motherhood never ceases once the child is conceived, but these two women shared something far more significant that day. Mary and Elizabeth shared the realization that they would play very central roles in the accomplishment of redemption. And Elizabeth knew that her own role paled in significance compared to the mother of God (Lk 1:43). No wonder Mary's soul magnified the Lord. Wouldn't you?

God revealed to Elizabeth what he wants each of us to embrace. That's why we are told that Elizabeth spoke by the prompting of the Holy Spirit. We too must recognize God coming to us in Mary's womb, an act that eclipses even our greatest personal joys. Why must we say with Elizabeth that Mary is most blessed of all women? Because our greatest happiness in life rests not on earthly joys, but in receiving Jesus into our homes and lives. We are most blessed among all people, just as Israel was, if we see God's dwelling among us as the center of our joy. As in the Old Testament, God does not dwell in thin air. He comes to us through the tangible things of this world such as a tabernacle or a temple. He comes to us through his servants. Elizabeth immediately recognized God's presence in Mary. Mary is the most blessed of women because she had experienced the dwelling of God within herself. She experienced what we all will experience in eternity, "Now the dwelling of God is with men, and he will live with them. They will be his people, and God himself will be with them and be their God." (Rev 21:3). The Holy Spirit within Elizabeth recognized the Holy One within Mary. If we are listening to the Spirit of God, if we are filled with God's presence like Elizabeth, we will spontaneously say of Mary, "blessed are you among women."

Mary, the Shepherds and the Birth of Jesus (Luke 2:1-20)

Only Luke gives us the events of the actual night of Jesus' birth so we must pay special attention to the details of his account to appreciate our Lord's first night in the world. To all human appearance the birth of a Jewish boy in the quiet recesses of the Judean hills of the first century could hardly be called spectacular. Yet the very note that Luke strikes is a universal one, a sound that heralds the worldwide impact of this birth. He tells us that Jesus was born in the time of the census decreed by Caesar Augustus when Quirinius was governor of Syria (Lk 2:1,2). Historians have long wrestled with the dating of Jesus' birth because of the apparently conflicting data. I will leave those issues to others. What seems clear is that Luke places Jesus' birth in this global context for a specific purpose.

Luke realized what his mentor Paul had preached, that Christ came not only to redeem Israel but to bring salvation to the world. As he reflected on this truth for many years, Luke no doubt wanted us to see an obscure birth of a baby boy as the center of the world. So he placed this birth in the context of world history. Jesus would have a global ministry, a cosmic impact, and what better way to signal that truth than to place the timing of his birth within the movement of the most powerful imperial machinery of that day, the Roman Empire. But there's more.

The visit of the shepherds signals that Jesus's birth is more than a global event on earth. Even the heavens are enlisted to proclaim how nothing will remain untouched by this birth. The angels appear to lowly shepherds who receive the heavenly message with joy and humility. What could be more different, more odd than the union of pure celestial messengers and poor shepherds! Yet this is precisely the significance of Jesus' birth, that the King of the angels has come to visit and minister to shepherds. Surely he who was rich became poor for our sake that we might be enriched by his poverty (cf. 2 Cor 8:9). The actual message of the angels declares the union of heaven and earth, *glory to God in the highest and on earth peace among men of his good pleasure* (Lk 2:14). The birth of Christ yields maximum glory to God in heaven and ushers in the peace of God's kingdom.

Mary contemplated all this — the worldwide scope of her Son's saving life, the union of heaven and earth, the humble worship of poor shepherds, not to mention all the glorious truths she had learned earlier — she drank in all the meaning of these events for her life, and that of her Son and husband. *But Mary, for her part, treasured all these words contemplating them in her heart.* (Lk 2:19). The verb translated *treasure up* (*suntereo*) means *to guard, to keep safe.* Luke uses the verb in the imperfect tense and it could be translated, "Mary kept guarding all these things in her heart." Mary didn't simply think about these events on occasion. She devoted her life to them. She turned them over again and again in her thoughts. She mused over them. She penetrated their depths. She lingered in their holy precincts. She drew on their holy power.

Mary is a model of a Christian who contemplates the holy mysteries. The term *mystery* is not well understood by Christians. In popular parlance, mystery is an event we don't understand because we don't have enough information, such as a murder mystery. Once the relevant information is supplied, we understand how the event happen and we "solve" the mystery. But this meaning is very far from its usage in a Christian context. *Mystery* in Christian history is an event (e.g. Jesus' birth) or truth (e.g. Trinity) whose meaning we *do* understand but whose depths we could never plumb. It is a mystery precisely because we do understand it. It baffles us because it is too good to be true. Knowledge of a mystery is more like knowing a person than knowing a mathematical equation. My wife and I have been married a little over twenty-three years. Even though we knew one another when we first married, our knowledge of one another now overshadows that earlier experience of knowledge. Our present experience is so much deeper and full of intimacy. Yet the more we know one another, the more we realize how far we still have to go. It seems that no matter how deeply we know one another, one will never fully comprehend the other. If this is true on a human level, how much more is it true of God.

Paul speaks of the *mystery of Christ* in Ephesians 3:4. This pithy expression means that the entirety of Christ's life, the whole incarnation, is a mystery. It is the mystery *of Christ* because he is the subject of the mystery *and* because Christ is the one who gave it. Luke 2:19 teaches that Mary contemplated the mystery of Christ. She no doubt realized that the gift of her Son was also the Giver of the gift. She meditated on the entire scope of his incarnate life. She understood it, but she still sat in awe before its ineffable depth. Could Mary have also understood what Paul says about the mystery of Christ in Ephesians 3:6? Could she see with her eye of faith that the Gentiles would be *fellow heirs, joined in the same body, and fellow partakers of the promise in Christ Jesus*? Could she possibly have seen that the union of her Son and her Son's Church was also a mystery (Eph 5:32)? She knew she was the mother of the Redeemer. Could she possibly be the mother of the redeemed? If her Son's church was as intimately united to him as she was, how could she be separated from that church, either as member or as mother? One thing seems clear: whatever Mary contemplated on the night of her Son's birth, she knew her Son was destined for a universal ministry of salvation. And she knew her own life was destined to be bound up with his. His life had cosmic significance and so hers must have the same.

Joseph and Mary Present Jesus in the Temple
(Luke 2:21-38)

Mary's life continued to be one of obedience after Jesus was born. Luke stresses how Joseph and Mary were faithful to the law of Moses by circumcising him on the eighth day and by dedicating him to God. Yet this dedication was like that of no other Jewish boy. This presentation was accompanied by the witness of two elderly servants of God, Simeon and Anna. Why did Luke recount this incident beyond the obvious fact that it was historically true? Part of the answer must be the Old Testament requirement that the truth of any matter demanded the confirmation of two or three witnesses (Dt 17:6). Simeon and Anna function as witnesses to the redemptive ministry that this child will have. For whom are they witnesses? The most likely answer is for Joseph and Mary. There's no evidence in the story that anyone else heard Simeon's words. Surely, Joseph and Mary already knew that their Son was the Savior of the world! Yet we forget how easy it would have been for Joseph and Mary to lose faith. Yes, they had been told many of the wonderful things their Jesus would do, but that was precisely the problem. Those things were so wonderful that they bordered on the unbelievable. They both needed constant assurance that their calling to be the parents of the world's Redeemer was from God. Normal parenthood requires heroic faith. How much more being parents of the Son of God!

Simeon's song of praise in Luke 2:29-32, traditionally called the *Nunc Dimittis*, reflects the longing of this old man's heart. Now he has seen "the consolation of Israel" (Lk 2:25) Now he knows that Israel will be redeemed and that is enough for him. Like Mary's *Magnificat*, Simeon's song weaves together quotations from the Old Testament to emphasize the universal scope of the Messiah's salvation.

> Now dismiss your servant, O Sovereign Lord
> According to your word.
> For my eyes have seen your salvation
> Which you prepared in sight of all peoples
> A light for revelation to the Gentiles
> And the glory of your people Israel. (Lk 2:29-32)

We will see in Chapter Four the great promises of the prophets that God's redemption would extend to the whole earth in the day of the Messiah's coming. This child will not only save Israel but will become a "light of revelation for the Gentiles" (Lk 2:32). We must appreciate how difficult it would have been for the average Jewish man or woman of the first century to believe that God would extend his salvation to the world. We can see that difficulty when we look at Peter's reluctance later in the Book of Acts (ch 10). Yet the universal scope of Jesus' salvation is centerstage for Mary and Joseph as they presented Jesus in the temple.

The story of the presentation also adds another truth that Joseph and Mary had to learn, that their exalted calling as Jesus' parents involved suffering. Simeon's message mixes joy and sadness, happiness and sorrow. This child's life will be the salvation of God's people, but he will also be the occasion of many to reject the Lord. He will cause *the rising and falling of many in Israel* and will be a *sign spoken against* (Lk 2:34). The pattern of acceptance and rejection can be found throughout biblical history. When God comes to save his people, some among his people choose to reject him. Not every Hebrew left Egypt; some stayed behind. And the prophets warned that the Messiah would be the one whom many would reject. All this implies the sufferings of the Messiah.

Simeon tells Mary specifically that the sufferings and pains of her Son will affect her directly. *A sword will pierce your very soul that the thoughts of many hearts may be revealed.* (Lk 2:34,35). It's perhaps significant that Joseph is not told this. This is not to minimize Joseph's role as the foster-father of our Lord, but only that the intense suffering of the soul will affect Mary more directly because she alone gave of her own body to the Son of God. Mary will join her Son in his sufferings as he redeems the world. His fate will be her fate. His joys will be hers, but his experience of sorrow will also touch her heart.

A suffering Messiah was a stumbling block to many Jews and that same suffering Savior is still an obstacle for many Christians. They want Jesus as long as he can do something positive for them, but they recoil from him when he asks them to suffer. That's why Mary is given to us as an example. No one suffers like a mother when her child has been hurt. And no one has suffered more than Mary because she joined her heart to the greatest suffering the world has ever known. The wages of sin is death. What greater suffering could there be than the sins of the world placed upon Jesus. Mary could have recoiled from the pain she was promised, but the gospel record says she embraced her Son all the more. Jesus endured the sufferings of the world, and Mary endured them too as she joined in his sufferings.

The Magi's Great Discovery (Matthew 2:1-12)

I mentioned earlier that Matthew's Gospel focuses on Joseph rather than on Mary. The two Gospel writers are complimentary, but their different emphases show us that we cannot separate Mary from Joseph and neither of them from Jesus himself. Yet the visit of the Magi, celebrated on the Feast of the Epiphany, shows us how Matthew and Luke both announce the world-wide scope of Christ's salvation. The prophets of Israel predicted the spread of the Messiah's saving work to the whole earth. This message demands the universal (catholic) nature of the Church. The Church must be universal because Christ's salvation is universal. Matthew's inclusion of the Magi shows that the "Light of the Gentiles" is already shining in his infancy. And the Magi provide us with an example of how all people should come and adore the Savior of the world.

There are several other important themes in the Magi's adoration of Christ. Matthew stresses how Herod opposed the plan of God with a ruthless cunning that rivals the worst hatred of any ancient king. Jesus' birth engenders royal conflict because Herod rightly perceives it as a threat to his kingdom. Any Jew could have seen this if he knew the promises of the Messiah as King (see Ps 110, Ps 2). The Magi are not kings — despite the traditional hymn *We Three Kings* — but are rather ancient wisemen, a profession that gave advice to kings by reading the stars. The Magi are royal dignitaries, however, and their obeisance to the infant King is properly read by Herod as a declaration of the destruction of his kingdom. Christ's birth is the beginning of a new kingdom, one that will be universal in scope and call for total allegiance.

Matthew does not tell us any of Joseph's or Mary's inner thoughts (compare Luke 2:19). He does not even mention Joseph although the entire birth narrative in his Gospel revolves around him. The major actors in the story are the Magi of course. Yet when he comes to the point of their arrival at the Holy Family's house, Matthew says, "they found the child with Mary his mother." (Mt 2:11). To appreciate this phrase, we must understand the historical context of Matthew's readers. These early Christians probably knew the basic outline of Jesus' birth *before* Matthew wrote his Gospel. They may have already known about the visit of the Magi. There's nothing in the Bible nor historical documents to make us think that all the information in the Gospels was brand new to their first readers. In fact, history suggests the opposite. We know many stories about Jesus circulated in the early Christian communities before the Gospels were written. Luke tells us that the purpose of his Gospel is to set down accurately the account of Jesus' birth, suggesting that some stories about Jesus' life may have been inaccurate.

If Matthew's first readers had some exposure to the stories of Jesus' birth, part of his purpose was to instruct them further about the actual events. But Matthew also wanted them to apply the truths of Jesus' life to their own lives. This concern for application of the truth to daily life helps us realize that the story of the Magi functions on two levels. One is the historical narrative about what the Magi did. The other is what the Church Fathers called "moral interpretation" i.e. interpretation that applies to our lives and challenges us to holiness.

The main point of the visit of the Magi is that we, the readers, are to do exactly what the Magi did i.e. fall down and worship the child, opening before him all our gifts and treasures (Mt 2:11,12). But if we choose to worship the child Messiah, we must realize that it means entering his kingdom, an act that will bring us into conflict with the kingdoms of this world. In this same line of thinking, the statement *they found the child with Mary his mother* (v. 11) takes on a moral as well as an historical meaning. Like the Magi, we too are to enter Jesus' house and find him there. We must search diligently for the child who is our Savior. We must want him, love him and be willing to sacrifice everything for him. But the astonishing truth is that when we find Jesus, we find him with his mother Mary. Their lives are completely bound to one another and intertwined.

Jesus and Mary are inseparable. That is the most basic truth of all the Catholic Church teaches about Mary. The Church insists that *what God has joined together, let no mere human separate.* (Mt 19:6). And that is why the Catholic Church can no more relinquish its teachings on Mary than it can deny the inseparability of the marriage bond. Both are divine bindings. If the Church cuts the cord of God's binding, it relinquishes its own right to speak for God in the world. We've seen in Luke's Gospel how Mary's whole life was dedicated to her Son. In her heart, her whole existence was for his glory. So, it is more than a historical fact that Jesus was with his mother. He was always with her because she was always with him. The orthodox Christian has no difficulty understanding that Christ always was. He was "in the beginning with God ... and was God." (Jn 1:1). But how was Mary always with Jesus? She was there in his eternal plan before the world began. She was prepared by God in her very conception in her mother's womb. Her heart was being readied by the Holy Spirit to receive the Son of God in her womb. When the Magi found the child with his mother, they only discovered what had been true, but hidden, from the beginning. So they worshipped him. When we worship Jesus, we worship him alone, as the Magi did, for he alone is God. Jesus alone on earth is God but Jesus is never alone. Jesus alone is worshipped but Jesus is with his mother Mary. We worship Him. We honor her as the one who brought him to us.

Jesus and the World's Hatred (Matthew 2:13-23)

Matthew's theme of kingdoms in conflict continues in the story of the flight into Egypt. Herod's anger and thirst for power knew no bounds as he seeks to do away with the rival to his throne. Before Jesus is ever able to speak a word, his kingdom threatens to undo the kingdoms of this world. Someday the kingdoms of this world will become the kingdoms of our Lord and of his Christ (cf. Rev 11:15). That day is foreshadowed in the story of Herod's treachery against the Holy Family.

God's mercy and protection cover Jesus and Mary through the dreams that are revealed to Joseph (Mt 2:13,19). Joseph takes center stage in this story as he protects and cares for the child and his mother. Joseph, the righteous man, performs the role assigned to him by God in the same humility that characterized Mary's life. Just as Mary said YES to God in conceiving God's Son, so Joseph said YES to God in his divine task of protecting the Savior of the world.

Why does the angel instruct them to go to Egypt? Surely other places closer would have been sufficient to protect them from Herod's hatred. The key is in the quotation from Hosea 11:1 found in Mt 2:15, *Out of Egypt have I called my son.* The escape to Egypt fulfills prophecy, a prominent theme in Matthew's way of telling about Jesus' life. How does this action fulfill prophecy? Hosea 11:1 looked back to the Exodus from Egypt when Yahweh's rescue of Israel was told in terms of the first-born son. Israel is God's first-born (cf. Ex 4:22). Yet Hosea's words were also applicable to the future exodus when God would bring his first-born out of Egypt for the second and last time. Jesus and Israel are both first-born sons because Jesus is the perfect Israel. The Father begins his final redeeming acts through the actions of his infant son. Joseph and Mary cooperate with God's plan of redemption by the role each of them plays in the story.

It is significant for our understanding of Mary that she is referred to as Jesus' mother in this account. When Jesus was not yet born, Matthew refers to Mary as Joseph's wife (1:20,25) but afterwards she is mentioned only as the child's mother. Three times it says that Joseph "took the child and his mother" (2:14,20,21). Again, Mary's significance comes from the relationship that she has with Jesus. The focus is on Jesus of course. Normally, we would expect it to be worded, Joseph took Mary and the child. But since the child is the focus of the story, Matthew reverses the normal order and speaks of the "child and his mother." Mary recedes into the background, a role that she no doubt wanted since her humility pointed to the greatness of her Son (cf. Lk 1:48) As the handmaid of the Lord, she knew her task in life was totally attached to Jesus.

Mary's Growing Faith: Jesus' Bar-Mitzvah (Luke 2:40-52)

The New Testament is silent about Jesus' years from infancy to the age of twelve, another fact that indicates how the inspired writers have selected certain events to portray our Lord in selected hues and tones. It is significant that of all the events of Jesus' life before the age of thirty, the one chosen teaches us much about Joseph and Mary. Jesus's bar-mitzvah at age twelve shows how Mary advanced in her pilgrimage of faith. Her faith was no static belief that needed no development. She had understood from Gabriel that her Son would be the Savior of the world, but she surely did not comprehend all that this entailed. Luke no doubt chose to tell us of Jesus' bar-mitzvah because it indicated his transition from boyhood to manhood. Yet his account of the story also emphasizes that Mary and Joseph had much to learn of Jesus' eventual mission.

Mary takes the lead role in their encounter with Jesus when they return to Jerusalem and find him in the temple conversing with the teachers of the law. It is Mary who asks, *why have you done this to us?* (Lk 2:48) Normally, it would have been expected that the man of the home would speak under such public circumstances. As we have seen, Luke focuses our attention on Mary. Though full of grace and showing that humility of heart which allowed her to cooperate with God's plan, Mary still didn't fully grasp the intimate link with Jesus' earthly life and his resolve to do the will of his heavenly Father (Lk 2:50). What she still had to learn was how absorbed Jesus must be in the divine will. This is why Jesus responded to her, *didn't you know that I had to be in my Father's house?* (Lk 1:49) This rather traditional translation is possible, and yet lacks something of the power of the original Greek. A better translation might be: *didn't you know that I must be about the things of my Father?*, or *didn't you know that I must be absorbed in the things of my Father?* The grammatical construction is the same as Paul uses when he commands Timothy: *Be absorbed in them* (I Tim 4:15). It indicates a total commitment to those things which belong to the Father. The language of Luke 1:49 foreshadows what Jesus would later tell his disciples, *My food is to do the will of Him who sent me and to finish His work* (Jn 4:34).

Mary had taught her Son as a boy, and now, on the verge of his manhood, he taught her one more lesson in obedience. She had willingly submitted to the Father's plan, but now she had to offer up her Son in obedience again so that he might be totally devoted to the Father's will. To accomplish God's work, Jesus had to be totally absorbed in the things of his Father. Mary too would have to follow in the footsteps of the One who had followed her steps in childhood.

A Woman for Our Times

Mary of Nazareth seems on the surface to be an ordinary Jewish woman whose life was indistinguishable from many others.

She cooked, sewed and cleaned. She prayed, conversed and served the needs of her family. Yet what we have already seen in the biblical stories of Jesus' birth shows that Mary's life was extraordinary. Her extraordinariness did not lie in herself; it was a divine gift. By the free choice of God the Father, she was predestined to be the mother of the Redeemer. By his mercy, the heavenly Father filled her soul with his grace and his presence. In divine providence, Mary became the Spouse of the Holy Spirit by receiving in her womb the Son of God. In the silence of her Son's infant life, she contemplated the astounding truths of heaven. This contrast between the ordinary and the extraordinary is important. The significance of Mary's life was hidden from everyday view. Rarely could others around her see the remarkable power and meaning of her life just as many could see nothing remarkable about the life of her Son. And Mary precedes us all in that same respect. Paul says our life is also hidden with Christ in God (Col 3:3,4). Our outward life may seem very ordinary, but the inner strength of our life is the same as Mary's. The source of that strength is the One whom Mary bore — the Savior of Bethlehem.

We share so much with Mary. Like her, we are called to be disciples of her Son. When she and Joseph found Jesus in the temple, they both learned more of what being disciples meant. It means giving over to God the Father the things in our lives which are most precious to us. But discipleship is impossible without faith, and Mary's example of faith calls us to the same commitment. When she says YES to God (Lk 1:38), she calls us to faith in Christ by her example. Faith also means walking with God in the dark times when we can't see where the road ahead is leading. Mary knew that experience by her hidden life. She won no awards and received no acclaim from the world in her day. Yet her hidden life was brimming with importance and power. Though her life appeared insignificant, her greatest influence came through the suffering she would endure. Simeon's words in Luke 2:35 call us to the same life as Mary's — a life of blessing through suffering. And not just any suffering. Her suffering and ours must be united with and flow from the sufferings of Mary's Son. Mary's Lord and ours.

We must recognize that while we are like Mary in many ways,

she is also unique. The Mother of Jesus became a unique channel of Christ's bodily presence in the world. Through her body the Son of God, indeed God himself, took his shape and form. Her eyes, her face, her stature, her blood, her DNA. Whatever natural makeup his body had, it came from this Blessed Virgin. We can never give to Jesus what Mary gave to him. She cooperated in God's plan of salvation in a unique way. We can never give the substance of our bodies to Jesus the way Mary did, but we can do what others around Mary did. We can welcome Jesus into our lives, our world, our businesses, our homes, our schools and our hearts. We can welcome both the Son of God into our lives, and his mother who is blessed above all women (Lk 1:42). Imagine yourself to be Simeon and you see the salvation of Israel (Lk 2:30,31). Would it have been possible to hail the One who would redeem the world, and not also call his mother blessed among women? Don't we call them happy, even blessed, who receive great gifts from God? Isn't Mary then the most blessed person to have ever lived? She received *in her own body* the greatest gift that anyone has ever received.

Mary is an instrument of the presence of God. She is a tabernacle where the Son of God came to dwell in the midst of his people (cf. John 1:14). Throughout this book we will look at the experience and promise of God's presence in the Old Testament among the people of Israel because it is there that we learn of God's yearning to live among his people. When the people of Israel were in the desert and saw the pillars of cloud by day and of fire by night, they bowed down and worshipped the Lord who had come to visit them with his special, local presence (Ex 33: 9,10). The same experience happened at the birth of Jesus. Matthew tells us that the Magi "found the child with Mary his mother." Their response was like that of the ancient Israelites who encountered the presence of God directly. "They fell down and worshipped him" (Mt 2:11). The Magi didn't simply feel God's general presence around them. They came to a specific place where God had given his presence in a specific way. They worshipped an infant boy who was God's presence made specific and local. They did not worship Mary just as the Israelites did not worship the tabernacle itself. But the Magi did honor Mary with their gifts because they recognized that she was the instrument of bringing God's presence into the world. Our goal as Christians is to find those places where God manifests his presence in our times, and to go there with the expectation of worshipping Him and of honoring those who are the instruments of his presence. God transforms and unifies his people by giving them his presence. And God's presence, once it fills the hearts of God's people, brings unity in their relationships with one another. I believe that if we recognize Mary as God's chosen instrument of unity for Christians, we would see a level of spiritual life and unity among Christians unprecedented in the last four hundred years of western Christianity.

CHAPTER TWO

MARY IN THE
MINISTRY OF JESUS

The course of Mary's life was set from the moment Gabriel appeared to her, but even she could not know how much her mission of giving the Son of God to the world would demand of her. In the previous chapter, we traced Mary's life up to Jesus' twelfth year. Now we will examine Mary's involvement in Jesus' public ministry from the age of thirty. We will see clearly that the truths announced in Jesus' birth and early life are continued and expanded in his later ministry, a fact that has profound implications for our understanding of Mary.

Chapter One focused heavily on the Gospels of Matthew and Luke, the only two that give any detail concerning the birth of Jesus. In this chapter, we will include Mark and John in our discussion with a special focus on John. John presents us with only two passages in his Gospel, but each reveals a wealth of information about Mary. To understand Mary properly, we will have to attend very carefully to the depth of each text that includes her.

The Gospel of John, like the other Gospels, is an intricately constructed literary piece which is not a biography of Jesus in the straightforward sense of a chronological treatment of his life. Each Gospel contains a "theology" i.e. an interpretation of Jesus' life designed to teach God's people some aspect of truth about our Lord. The four Gospels then are like looking at the life of Christ through a kaleidoscope. If you turn it, you see the same object through different lenses. Each Gospel contributes its own divinely inspired perspective on Christ's life. John's selection of events is so unique that we must ask what purpose each story has in his Gospel. For example, the raising of Lazarus in chapter eleven points to Jesus as the resurrection and the life (Jn 11:25). Similarly, the feeding of the multitudes in chapter six points to Jesus as the bread of life (Jn 6: 35). The reader, like the original disciples, is called to faith in Jesus as the Son of God. This clearly reflects the purpose of the Gospel as spelled out in the opening prologue, "As many as received him, He gave to them authority to be become the children of God, to those who believe on His name." (1:12). A more explicit statement of the same theme occurs toward the conclusion of the Gospel, "These things have been written that you may believe that Jesus is the Christ, the Son of God and that believing you may have life in His name." (John 20:31). The entire Gospel of John is designed to lead the reader to faith in Jesus as the Son of God. Consequently, we are told that not everything in Jesus' life and ministry has been included (20:30). How does Mary's role in the Gospel of John lead to faith in Jesus?

Mary and Jesus at the Wedding Feast (John 2:1-11)

We meet Mary for the first time in John's Gospel at the wedding feast of Cana where Jesus turns the water into wine. John stresses the significance of this event in the last verse, "Jesus did the first of his signs in Cana of Galilee and manifested his glory, and his disciples believed on Him." (Jn 2:11) How does the miracle of turning water into wine lead us to see Jesus' glory and increase our faith in him? The account of the wedding feast has several prominent themes, but one of the most important is the relation between Jesus and Mary in the story. John tells us that "Mary was there while Jesus and his disciples were invited to come." (Jn 2:1,2). Mary was probably there because she had some personal friendship with the wedding couple. She did not need to be invited because she was already a part of the wedding festivities. She was not a guest, properly speaking, but played an integral role in the celebration itself.

Jesus' presence at the wedding is highlighted by his being invited. He is there as a bystander, as it were, and is drawn by Mary into solving the young couples' problem. This occasion underscores a theme elsewhere in John's Gospel, that of the *provision which Jesus makes*. Jesus producing the wine is a revelation of his glory because it foreshadows his giving of his life for the salvation of his sheep (cf. John 10:11). A second theme is the *surprise at the quality of wine* which Jesus gives. In the Old Testament wine is symbolic of joy and this association is probably behind John's account. Jesus' wine makes us glad far above our expectations.

Perhaps the most important theme is hidden in the words, "my hour has not yet come." (Jn 2:4). John attaches special significance to the coming of Jesus' hour. What does this phrase mean? John 13:1 gives us the clue, "Before the Passover feast, Jesus knew that his hour had come to pass from this world to the Father ..." This verse opens the final stage of Jesus' ministry in John's Gospel so that *his hour* is the time of his suffering, death and resurrection, events that represent the consummation of his saving work on earth. When Jesus tells Mary, "my hour has not yet come," he teaches her that this is not the time for the glorification of the Son of Man. He should not reveal his glory, not yet anyway. Jesus' words may imply that Mary knew that her Son would reveal his glory through his suffering, death, and resurrection. Given the events of his early life, it wouldn't be surprising. She knew what he had to do, but she didn't understand *when* it was to be done. The statement in verse 11 is interesting in this light. It says Jesus "revealed his glory, and his disciples believed on him." It is as if the performing of the miracle could not hold back the glory and splendor of the Son of God. The miracle cracked open the door, and the glory came flooding through.

If this wasn't the hour for Jesus' glory to be revealed, why did he perform the miracle at that time? One reason may be Mary herself. She never actually makes a direct request; she only points out that there is no wine (v3). But Jesus takes it as a request for a miracle. Even though this is not the hour for him to reveal his glory, his mother's request moves him to act in the couples' behalf. This helps us understand the seemingly negative tone of Jesus' words. Jesus seems to put Mary off with his words, "What is there between you and me, woman? My hour has not yet come" (2:4). In English, to use *woman* in this way seems denigrating; the problem is with English, not the original Greek. The *New International Version* offers a good translation showing Jesus' respect for his mother, "Dear Lady." But *woman* is also used of Mary in John 19:26. There may also be an allusion to Eve here as the *woman* of Genesis. As Adam and Eve cooperated with one another in bringing sin into the world, so Jesus and Mary are cooperating as the New Adam and the New Eve to bring Jesus' glory into the world.

What then is the meaning of his question "What have you to do with me?" (RSV). The original Greek is *ti emoi kai soi* which is probably built on the Semitic model *ma li va leka*. This literally means "What is there between you and me?" but the question may not be a rebuff at all. Its meaning might be paraphrased as follows:

> what does this request mean to me and what does it mean to you? Does it mean the same to you as it does to me? You come with a common problem about wine. There is more involved than you realize. To perform a miracle entails a revelation of my glory (cf 2:11). The hour for the full revelation of my glory is not yet here.

Jesus' question then is not putting Mary off but is challenging her to rethink her relationship to him. Thus, what Mary says in response follows naturally from Jesus' words. She commands the servants to do whatever her Son commands because now she has come to a new and deeper understanding of his redemptive mission. Mary realizes that now is not the time for his full glory to be revealed, but he also concedes her request because of his infinite love for his mother.

Why then is Mary a prominent figure in this wedding feast at Cana? As the mother of Jesus she is in a unique position to show us the glory of her Son. She can instruct us in the lessons of obedience because she has come to understand the heart of her Son. The inclusion of Mary in the wedding feast is to emphasize the authority of Jesus. We are still to hear her say to us, "Do whatever He tells you." From Mary's body comes the gift of God; from her lips comes the command of God. Her role is to lead us to be obedient Christians. Like the first readers of John's Gospel, we must see the glory of

Jesus shown through his miracles, but we must not be like those who followed Jesus only because their stomachs were filled (cf. John 6:26). Rather, we must see Jesus' signs as revealing a heavenly glory that is uniquely his own. Mary's role is to teach us that once we have seen Jesus' glory, we must also walk in obedience to him.

Mary at the Cross of Jesus (John 19:25-27)

At the end of Jesus' life on earth, we find Mary at the cross. It is the only other place in John's Gospel where we find the mother of Jesus in addition to the wedding feast of Cana. On one level, the close devotion of his mother is understandable. Every mother would be at her son's death, but the story goes beyond natural motherly compassion. John provides us with a beautiful and tender picture of Mary at the feet of Jesus, showing her loving consent to the offering of Jesus as victim for our sins. Mary offered her Son as an act of supreme charity. The two appearances of Mary at Cana and at the cross emphasize her role as the mother of Jesus. Her personal name is never used in John's Gospel because it is her role as mother that is most important. By her appearance at the beginning of his public ministry and at his crucifixion, John stresses her cooperation in the redemptive work which Jesus performs. By her presence at the cross, she openly proclaims not only her maternal love, but her willingness to be her Son's disciple. And John 19:25-27 also tells us what Jesus thinks of his mother. The story of the wedding feast at Cana showed us *what Mary can teach us about Jesus*; the story of Mary at the cross shows *what Jesus can teach us about his mother*.

For years I saw nothing more in Mary's presence at the cross than its historical factualness and the concern of Jesus for his mother. Yet John's account of the crucifixion suggests that more is intended. If Jesus came to reveal the glory of the Father and to complete his work on the cross, an important part of his redemptive work is entrusting his disciples to his mother's care. This is why the Church Fathers saw more in this text than a simple historical event. Their perceptions of John's literary craft were amazingly accurate.

John's literary artistry is evident on several levels. He often uses words that can be understood on a simple ordinary level and also on a more profound one. The clearest example is when Caiaphas the high priest declares that it is expedient for one man to die for the whole nation. Caiaphas understands his own words to mean only that it would be better for Jesus to die instead of the whole nation dying (Jn 11:50). But John tells us that when Caiaphas said this, "he prophesied that Jesus would die for the nation [Jews]. And not only for the nation but that all the scattered children of God that they might be brought into one." (Jn 11:51,52). The words have one meaning for Caiaphas and another for the reader. John wants us to understand Jesus' death in a much more profound sense than physical death.

John does the same in his account of the crucifixion. He emphasizes the completeness of several actions in the story. Pilate's words, "What I have written, I have written" (19:22) are a reminder of the official status of the proclamation which hung over Jesus' head. Pilate understood the words as meaning only that he wouldn't change what he had written. We as readers are to understand that Jesus is proclaimed the King of the Jews (19:21) in spite of his enemies. The truth of Jesus's Kingship cannot be changed or repressed. Jesus also says, "It is finished" (19:30). On one level it simply means that his life is over. On a deeper level, it means that the definitive act of redemption he came to perform has now been completed. So, John's use of words is often more subtle and powerful than appears on the surface, a fact that becomes important in the words of 19:26.

Let's also look at John's literary genius in telling the story of Mary and the beloved disciple. John 19:25-27 cannot be divorced from the verses which immediately precede (vss 23-24) because the writer intentionally connects the story of the soldiers dividing Jesus' garments with that of Mary at the cross. This is evident at the end of v24 when John says, "on the one hand, the soldiers did these things, but, on the other hand, standing there next to the cross of Jesus were Mary etc." This structure (*men* = on the one hand ... *de* = on the other hand) connects the two stories by way of contrast. John wishes to contrast the callous and cavalier treatment of Jesus by the four soldiers with the loving and devoted treatment of Jesus by the four women who are at Jesus' feet. And this contrast of four noble souls (the women) with four ignoble ones (soldiers) is complemented by John's dividing each story into two parts. First, the soldiers. Matthew, Mark and Luke all note that the soldiers divided Jesus' clothes by casting lots for them, each evangelist quoting Psalm 22:19 (see Mt 27:35; Mk 15:24; Lk 23:34). John, on the other hand, expands the story by saying that the soldiers "divided the clothes into four parts, one part for each soldier" (v23). Then the soldiers cast lots for the tunic. John makes two parts out of the event that was telescoped by the other three evangelists. Secondly, John divides the story of Jesus' words to his friends into two parts that correspond to the two parts of the soldiers' actions. Jesus performs his filial duty by entrusting his mother to the beloved disciple's care (behold your son). Then Jesus entrusts his disciple to his mother's care (behold your mother).

And there is a further relationship between each part of both stories. In the first part of the story of the soldiers, the theme is separation, that is, separating Jesus from his clothes and dividing them among the soldiers. In the first part of story of the women, the theme is also separation, but now in a more profound sense. It is the separation between Jesus and his mother. He now must commit his beloved mother to his beloved disciple. The theme of the second part of the story of the soldiers is unity. Vss 23,24 emphasize how the tunic was a whole piece and could not be divided. "Let's not tear it" said the soldiers. So too, the theme in the second part of Jesus' words is unity, but now in a more profound way than not tearing a simple tunic. Jesus' committing his disciple to his mother unifies Mary with the disciple.

What was John trying to convey with this intricate literary development? There is much more here than meets the eye. Before Jesus could leave this world and go into his kingdom (cf. 18:36), he had an important task to perform. This task had two sides. One was to entrust the care of his mother to his beloved disciple, John. The other was to entrust his disciple to his mother. Let's consider the first task. It is Jesus' filial duty. He must make provision for his mother, "Woman, here is your son" (Jn 19:26). As in the story of Cana, the use of the word *woman* evokes the memory of Genesis 3:15 where the woman is said to crush the head of the serpent. Mary has taken on that role. But why does

Jesus give the beloved disciple to his mother? You can almost hear a cruelty in these words. Mary's grief over her Son's mistreatment and his horrible crucifixion must have been overwhelming. How he could now point away from their relationship as mother and son to another person? It was because Mary has another important lesson to learn at the bitter end of her Son's life. This is a lesson that goes beyond the simple historical meaning of the words. We can understand the words, "here is your son" as intended only for Mary and the beloved disciple but that would be to take them as Caiaphas took his own words i.e. in a physical sense only. John no doubt wants us to understand them in the more profound sense of Mary adopting everyone that the beloved disciple represents, that is, every Christian. Jesus wants Mary to realize now that her motherhood extends beyond his physical life to the mystical life of his Church. She once cared for Christ's physical body; now she will care for Christ's church body.

"Here is your mother" Jesus says to the beloved disciple. This is Jesus' way of telling his disciple that the loving care the Master showed in his earthly life will continue in the person of his mother. The solemnity and finality of this act underscores the ancient belief that now Mary's maternal role is fulfilled, not only in the unique Son of God, but also in Jesus' brothers and sisters in the Church. How do we know this was Jesus' (and John's) meaning? By the phrase, "beloved disciple." Ancient Christian belief and modern scholarship agree that John used this title of himself. The "beloved disciple" is the author. Why did he not use his name? For the same reason that Mary is not called by her name, but called "the mother of Jesus." It is her role as mother that's important. Similarly, John wants us to see that it's not his own person that's important. He is representative of every Christian. Every Christian is a "beloved disciple" of Jesus. On the simple historical level, this phrase means that John was supposed to take Mary and care for her as if she were his own mother. On a deeper level, the reader should put himself in the place of the beloved disciple and hear Jesus saying, "here is your mother."

John 19:27 tells us what the proper response is, "from that hour the disciple took her as his own." At a purely historical level, this means that John took Jesus' mother into his care and provided for her physical needs. But recall the two levels of meaning that the author of this Gospel often intends. The wording of the verse invites us to understand more. The verb translated "took" also means "received"— a verb often used in John's Gospel to indicate faith in Christ (cf. 1:12). Also the phrase that I translated "as his own" is significant. It is usually translated, "into his own home" but this is an interpretation that is not authoritative. The phrase in Greek, *eis ta idia* can indicate a more personalized reception so that John's action is much deeper than physical care. It is exactly the same phrase used by John in 1:11 when he says that Jesus "came unto his own (*eis ta idia*) but his own did not receive him." 1:11 does not mean that Jesus came to his own house but that Jesus came to his very own people i.e. the Jews. So, what does the phrase mean in 19:27? It means that John received Mary as his very own mother, just as Jesus commanded him. He took her not only in a physical sense; he received her into his heart. We are asked to do the same. *As beloved disciples of the Lord, we should also receive Mary as our very own mother.*

The power of John's message is seen in the balance between Cana and the Cross. At the wedding feast of Cana, Mary speaks to reinforce Jesus' authority. She urges Christians to do whatever He tells us. At the Cross, Jesus speaks to reinforce Mary's mother-hood. He urges Christians to receive Mary into their lives with the words, "Here is your mother." This sorrowful scene says some-thing essential about our Christian lives in this world. The cross is the central, most important event in history because Jesus' cruci-fixion was the payment for our sin that we owed to God. John's emphasis falls on how Jesus ministers to his disciples to the very end of his life. This scene is a living demonstration of what John already told us, that Jesus "because he loved his own who were in the world, he loved them to the end." (John 13:1). But how does Jesus show his love for us? By doing two acts that dovetail into one. At the moment of his death Jesus gives us his life through the gift of his mother. We now become his brothers in a new sense because we have the same mother. All that remains is for us to take Mary into our lives as our spiritual mother.

Mary's Other Appearances in the Gospel Story

Mary never appears in other New Testament passages as prominently as she does in the ones I have discussed in Chapter One and in this chapter, but it is worth noting briefly those other texts because they have given rise to misunderstanding from time to time. The Gospel of Mark has no references to Jesus' birth. The only occasion in which Mary is mentioned is at the end of Chapter Three (Mk 3:31-35). The parallel passages in Mt 12:46-50 and Lk 8:19-21 don't differ significantly for our purposes. Some Christians have often thought that Jesus was distancing himself from his mother when he asked, "who are my mother and my brothers?" Our Lord goes on to define these relationships in the following way, "he who does God's will is my brother, my sister and my mother." (Mk3:35). Is Jesus saying that his relationship with his relatives is unimportant, even with his mother? Taken too strongly, one might see Jesus here as breaking the commandment to honor one's father and mother. Yet this text can hardly be taken as a denigration of his mother or other relatives. What does it mean?

Jesus is speaking about two types of family, one natural, the other supernatural. He and everyone are members of some human family, and Jesus does not deny membership in his own family. But Jesus' mission was to establish a new type of family. It is the new family of the supernatural order. The kingdom of God will not be based on blood descent but on obedience to the will of God. Is Jesus then putting down his mother and other relatives? Not at all. He is simply stressing that allegiance to the family of God in the kingdom of God must have the highest priority in our lives. Now, who are some examples of this new kind of familial relationship? Who demonstrates that membership in the supernatural family depends on obedience to the will of God? One of the greatest examples is Mary! Mary's words to Gabriel, "be it done to me according to your word." (Lk 1:38) are a perfect illustration of Jesus' statement in Mk 3:35, "whoever does the will of God is my brother, sister and mother." She was challenged to move from the natural relationship to the supernatural one. And she responded in true faith. Mary submitted herself to the will of God for her life.

The only other significant place we find Mary is with the apostles who are waiting on "the promise of the Father" i.e. the descent of the Holy Spirit on the infant church (Acts 1:14). As Mary was obedient to Gabriel's voice at the annunciation, so her obedience shows itself in her listening to the words of Jesus. With the leaders of the church she anticipates the empowerment of the church for the apostolic ministry. We saw in John 19:26 how the Lord Jesus gave his mother to the whole church symbolized in the beloved disciple John. Now we see the mother of the church in prayer with the apostles waiting on the same source of strength for the infant Body of Christ that created the real body of Christ within her own womb some thirty-three years earlier. Mary at prayer with the apostles portrays the beautiful family of God that was just beginning to be formed. Here were Jesus' brothers, sisters and his mother because these servants were "those who did the will of God." (cf. Mk 3:35).

Mary's Response and Ours

Mary's response to God's grace in her life helps us to understand that unity among Christians comes through faith and obedience. Mary is a sign, an indicator of how we must respond to God. What were Mary's responses? The most justly famous is her response to God's invitation through Gabriel, "behold the handmaiden of the Lord. Be it done to me according to your word." (Lk 1:38). With this commitment she showed herself to be Jesus' mother in both the natural and supernatural orders. It was a response prompted by grace and fulfilled by obedience. And obedience leads to praise. Mary praised her heavenly Father in the *Magnificat* (Lk 1:46-55) for the salvation that had dawned on the human race. Any parent knows the delight of having a child express thanks for favors done. Mary knew instinctively that the Father in heaven would be pleased with her song of thanksgiving. She wanted to give praise to him because she wanted to delight his heart.

What moved Mary to obedience and praise? Wasn't it her contemplative spirit? She constantly "treasured up these words" turning them over in her mind and heart again and again (Lk 2:19, 51). Mary knew what Paul would later write, that the life of her Son, the

Christ, was a mystery (see Col 1:24-2:3 esp. 2:2). Indeed, Christ's life contained "the mystery that was hidden for ages and generations, but now has been revealed to the saints" (Col 1:26). Mystery in the Bible is not a five dollar novel but a priceless revelation of the Father's glory (cf. Jn 1:14-18). Paul calls it a mystery because it is at once revealed and concealed. Concealed to the spiritually obtuse; revealed to those with open hearts. Since Mary's life was inseparably bound to Jesus, her life becomes a mystery just like his. In fact, their lives are not two separate mysteries but one grand mystery — the mystery of salvation. Jesus' life is the saving mystery and Mary was drawn into it by grace. That's why Mary's life is a sign of salvation, because her life is drawn into the mystery of her Son's life. Salvation is to be drawn into the love and power of the Son of God. Christ humbled himself to share in our humanity that we might share his divinity. Mary is a harbinger of our future.

Our response to Mary is indicated by how others around her responded to her extraordinary life. Those responses strike me as compelling because I looked on Mary as little more than the virgin-mother for the first forty years of my life. Mary was simply a biblical fact. Even then I never plumbed the depths of her virginity or maternity. But the responses to Mary in the Bible compel us because they provide wisdom and guidance on how we should respond to God's extraordinary work in her life. They compel us because they are responses to God's grace. And what does our salvation depend on? On how we respond to God's grace and salvation!

No better clue to our response can be found than Elizabeth's, John the Baptist's mother. Her spirit-filled words to Mary (cf Lk 1:41) should penetrate every Christian's heart, "blessed are you among women and blessed is the fruit of your womb" (Lk 1:42). We can scarcely imagine what it would be like for the mother of our Lord to come to our home as she carried God within her womb (Lk 1:43). We can and should be no less amazed than Elizabeth to have Mary in our lives. Simeon provides a further indicator of the proper response to Mary. For Simeon, the baby in Mary's arms was "the light of revelation for the Gentiles and the glory of Israel." The old prophet knew that this child was destined for "the falling and rising of many in Israel and a sign to be contradicted"

(Lk 2:34). But Simeon also knew that Mary's future life was so intimately bound to her Son's that he promised her, under the direct inspiration of the Spirit, that "a sword will also pierce her soul." (Lk 2:35). The future sufferings of Jesus would be so profuse that they would overflow into Mary's life. Her life would become a mirror of his life. Today, we can look upon Mary as a reflection of Jesus her Son. Mary is our window into the one and only Son of God who alone can unify people torn apart by misunderstanding and prejudice.

The Magi help us also respond to Mary. They found Jesus with his mother after a long and arduous search for the King of the Jews. They circumvented the murderous threats of a power hungry tyrant named Herod. When they found the Holy Family, they fell down and worshipped the child and honored his parents. The Magi call us to commitment, to leave our native land, and to search for Jesus. They call us to worship Jesus as the Savior of the world and to honor his mother as the one who gave Him to the world. But perhaps our most important response to Mary is guided by Joseph's. It is almost impossible to imagine the puzzlement and pain he must have felt when he learned that his espoused was pregnant (Mt 1:20). Yet Matthew's account shows clearly how Joseph obediently played the role that divine providence had set for him. In the quiet background, Joseph took his place in the kingdom of God to perform God's will no less than Mary. And his love for Mary and Jesus flowed from a truly just and holy heart (Mt 1:19). His love for his wife Mary was a perfect picture of Christ's love for the Church (cf Eph 5:29). It is the same love we are called to have for Jesus and Mary.

CHAPTER THREE

THE PROBLEM
OF CHRISTIAN UNITY

The first two chapters surveyed Mary's earthly life to discover what we could learn about her from the pages of Holy Scripture. Mary appears in Scripture to be intimately and inseparably bound to her Son Jesus Christ. She was more than just the human flesh through which the Divine Word entered the world. She was united to Christ in body and soul. And Jesus was also bound to her as her child, her Lord and the source of her life. She was the source of his human life and he was the source of the divine life that filled her life. This intimate union between Jesus and Mary is the foundation and basis of our hope that Christians can be unified. Unity is not an unfulfilled wish or an amorphous hope. Unity has both material and form, both substance and shape. Unity looks like a man and indeed is a man. Jesus alone is our unity, but Jesus is never alone. He is always with his mother.

The same Jesus that came from Mary's womb also founded a church and promised that the gates of hell would not be able to withstand the onslaught of the kingdom of God (Mt 18:18). The same Jesus that nursed at Mary's breast prayed for the unity of his followers in the garden on the night before his death (John 17). In this chapter we want to explore why Christians are not unified and how Scripture points us to a solution. We will see that unity among Christians cannot be achieved with means of our own contriving. Only by drawing deeply from the wellspring of Christ's own person can we hope to find the unity that Christ desires.

Christians are divided and Christ cannot be pleased. Our Lord prayed for the unity of his followers on the last night of his earthly life, a fact that shows how deeply he cares about the unity of his disciples (Jn 17:20ff). Why does Christ care if his people are one? In Chapter Four, we will see clearly that the Old Testament promised the unity of God's people when the Messiah came. That alone suggests that Jesus' ministry on earth had to fulfill one of the most important promises of the ancient Scriptures. If the people of God were not one, then Christ would have failed in his mission of salvation. Since there is only one Savior, there should be only one people who are saved. But why are Christians not one? If that was Jesus' intention, what went wrong?

In the college town where I live, Christian students recently had a "Jesus Night." This event was billed as an attempt for all the Christian groups on campus to lay down their differences and come together to worship Jesus. "Leave our differences at the door" was the cry. Apparently, the event was a big success because it met a felt need among the participants, the need to express our love for one another in Christ. This *Jesus Night* arose from a God-given sentiment, that of being one in Christ. But it also illustrates one of the thorniest problems facing Christians who seek to be unified in Christ. Doctrinal differences have divided Christians for centuries. The desire to be one and the need to believe the truth that Christ taught are both genuine inspirations from the Holy Spirit. But how does one balance these two important truths? My own personal struggles in this matter illustrate the problem that is deep and wide among Christians.

The Dilemma of Truth vs. Unity: A Personal Struggle

In May of 1977, I graduated from Westminster Theological Seminary in Philadelphia, Pennsylvania. I had spent three solid years in theological study that was intennded to prepare me for the Presbyterian ministry. One of my professors was Rev. Edmund Clowney, the president of the seminary, who taught a class on the doctrine of the church (ecclesiology). Professor Clowney spent a good amount of time addressing an urgent question he felt was being neglected by most evangelical Christians. From the Scriptures, Mr. Clowney urged on us the importance of the unity of the church. He saw quite clearly how fragmented evangelical Christians were and how much this situation contradicted our Lord's desire in John Chapter 17. His teaching sparked within me a desire for something I had seen in the Scriptures myself. During my college years, I had already been impressed with how Paul exhorted his readers in Corinth to be unified in doctrine and love (I Co. 1:10ff). By the end of seminary, I had already concluded on the basis of the New Testament that many different denominations were not the intention of Jesus Christ nor of his apostles. But I was at a loss to know what to do about the problem of divisions among Christians.

In 1978, I preached a sermon from John Chapter 17 at an ordination service of a fellow Presbyterian minister. I urged the congregation that day to seek unity among themselves. As I reflected on the intensity of our Lord's prayer recorded by John, I realized that Jesus would not be pleased with Christians who divided themselves from one another. I even went so far as to say that if the Roman Catholic Church ever came back to the Gospel of Jesus Christ, we must go back to it. At that time, I sincerely believed that the Catholic Church was not teaching the real Gospel.

The problem of disunity among Christians continued to haunt me for years. In 1988, I began teaching at a Protestant seminary. Although I was teaching Biblical Studies, I spent a lot of time reading church history, especially Protestant church history. I was working on a book on the history of science and religion in Protestant lands during the time of the Reformation. I had studied church history in seminary, but this time my reading revealed facts that astounded me. I discovered that within one hundred fifty years after Martin Luther first posted his ninety-five theses on the Wittenberg church door, the Protestant movement was hopelessly fragmented. In England alone, there were literally hundreds of groups who claimed their interpretations of the Bible and Christian doctrines were the correct ones. Some Protestant groups, especially the more independent ones, developed the idea of *the spiritual nature of the church*. They claimed that the institutional church was relatively unimportant and that the only necessary thing was for an individual believer to have a relationship with Jesus Christ. No Christian body in history has ever denied that a living relationship with Jesus Christ is necessary for salvation. The innovation of certain modern forms of Protestantism was that this was all that was important and that the institutional church must take a back seat. This same belief echoes down to our day: "It doesn't matter what church you belong to as long as you know Jesus." Whether they meant it or not, that was the message conveyed by the college students who held their *Jesus Night*.

As I studied my way through four hundred years of Protestant history, a pattern began to emerge that can be illustrated from twentieth-century Protestantism. In the early decades of this century, there arose the problem of liberalism or modernism, as some called it. Classic Protestant Liberalism said in essence that it was not important whether one believed in the historic doctrines of the Christian faith. In fact, one classic expression of this view reduced Christianity to three beliefs: (1) The fatherhood of God (2) the infinite value of the human soul and (3) the law of love to God and neighbor. Historic Christians — then called fundamentalists but with a different connotation than today — resisted this reductionism, and it led to serious splits among various Protestant denominations. In my own Presbyterian heritage alone, you can find dozens of splits and schisms among those who claim that others had left the faith.

I discovered that the problem facing the college students in my town has been repeated again and again throughout history. It is *the problem of truth vs. unity*. This problem poses an unsolvable dilemma for Christians who buy into it. And I unknowingly bought into it for many years. The problem comes down to this. If Christians choose to emphasize some aspect of Christian teaching as essential, then they end up separating from those who do not hold that teaching. On the other hand, if Christians attempt to be one in Christ and follow Christ's teaching on unity, then they must end up saying that certain teachings are not essential. The attempt is to include each group with different opinions while holding that those opinions are of little or no importance. This dilemma pits truth against unity, and requires us to choose either one or the other, but not both. The great challenge facing Christians today is how we can have *both truth and unity*.

For many years I could see no way out of this dilemma. The more specific some Christians become in their doctrines, the more other Christians had to be distanced from them in a visible manner. The only alternative was to deemphasize doctrine and to embrace as wide a group of Christians as possible. For the first group, right doctrine is one of the controlling marks or features of the church. If you don't have right doctrine, they say, you don't have a church. The second group takes unity without doctrine as the defining characteristic (mark) of the church. If you don't have unity with love, they say, you don't have a church. But such unity was at a great price. It has unity only by downplaying the importance of the content of the faith. How could this dilemma be overcome? As I read and reread the New Testament, it becomes clear to me that the apostles made no choice between doctrinal truth and unity. If the church is built on the foundation of the apostles and prophets, as Paul says in Ephesians 2:20, then only apostolic doctrine will protect against seriously wrong beliefs (heresy). And only apostolic unity will protect Christians from seriously wrong division (schism). In short, if the apostles were here today, they would not choose truth or unity. They would embrace *both* truth *and* unity.

The Problem of Unity in Paul's Letters

The dual problems of schism and heresy in the Church didn't begin with Protestantism. Schism is the act of wilfully separating from the Church. Heresy is teaching something that is contrary to the Gospel, the Scriptures and the teaching of Christ. Schism is a sin against love; heresy is a sin against truth. These problems began not more than twenty years after our Lord Jesus ascended into heaven. The New Testament writers themselves attest to the presence of false teachers within the Church. They also speak of those who have cut themselves off from the fellowship of the Church through attempts to break up the body of Christ (schism). In fact, many of the letters in the New Testament were written to handle precisely these two reoccurring problems.

Paul's letters to the Corinthians indicate severe problems involving a party spirit in the church and a denial of apostolic authority. In I Corinthians alone, Paul deals with schism (1:10-17), misunderstandings of his apostolic ministry (Chapters 3 & 4), problems of gross immorality (Chapters 5 & 6), marriage (Chapter 7), legalism (Chapter 8), liturgical abuses (Chapter 11), conflicts over spiritual gifts (Chapters 12-14), and denial of the resurrection (Chapter 15). This is a list that would keep a modern pastor busy for the rest of his life. What's most important for our purposes is his opening section on divisions in the church (I Cor 1:10-17).

We must place ourselves back into the position of Paul's original readers, if we are to understand his teaching. When Paul's letter arrived at Corinth, the people of the church there were divided along party lines that were identified by the names of various leaders.

> Each one of you says, "I belong to Paul" another says "I belong to Apollos" another says, "I belong to Cephas [Peter]. Still another says, "I belong to Christ." (I Cor 1:12)

The first three groups identified themselves with certain men as if their own leader had special access to the truth. For example, those who followed Paul denied that Apollos and Peter had the true Gospel. What about the last group, the Christ party? Maybe they were tired of all the denominations and decided just to follow Jesus pure and simple. To anyone who knows the history of Western Christianity over the past four hundred years, this is exactly what has happened again and again. Various leaders arise who don't intend to start a new denomination as such, but their followers begin to identify themselves almost completely with their leader. When these denominations fight with one another long enough, someone says, "Christ is lost in the confusion" and determines to get back to Jesus himself. These "Back to Jesus" movements inevitably distance themselves from other mere denominations with the confidence that they have some special access to the true Christ. The similarity between what happened in Corinth and modern Christianity is uncanny.

What is sadly striking is how modern Christians have completely ignored Paul's solution to this problem. Paul did not accept a denial either of truth or unity. Any lack of commitment to apostolic witness is a denial of truth. Any lack of unity in the Church is a denial of the one body of Christ. Let's look at Paul's words more closely.

> I appeal to you, brothers, through the name of our Lord Jesus Christ that you all agree and that there be no divisions [schisms] among you but that you would be knit together in the same mind and the same opinion. (I Cor 1:10).

Paul categorically rejects the possibility of divisions in the church. The strength of his conviction is shown by his phrase, *through the name of our Lord Jesus Christ.* When Paul makes his appeal through Jesus' name, he exercises the apostolic authority that comes from Christ himself. To appeal through Christ's name is to command through Christ's character. There must be no divisions in the church because Christ is one and his honor is at stake. The existence of divisions in the church contradicts the nature of the church and of Christ himself. "Is Christ divided?" Paul asks in verse 13. Of course not. Given what Paul teaches in verse 10, it is beyond comprehension how any Christian could ever justify leaving the church and starting a new one.

What kind of unity is Paul urging here? Precisely the most difficult kind to achieve, doctrinal unity. Paul's solution is not to urge love at the expense of truth but *unity in truth.* His words are, "that you all agree ... and ... that you would be knit together in the same mind and the same opinion." Agreement means literally saying *the same thing. The same mind* means agreeing in beliefs and teachings. The idea that there could be unity among Christians without doctrinal unity is completely foreign to Paul's thinking. This is why Paul asks some rhetorical questions in verse 13: "Has Christ been divided? Paul was not crucified for you, was he? Or, were you baptized in Paul's name?" To divide the church is to attempt to divide Christ since the church is the body of Christ. Baptism signifies and imparts Christ to the recipient so baptism in any other name is impossible for a Christian. Paul's teachings are clear. The church cannot be divided so Christians must embrace Christ's church without divisions and must be unified in both love and doctrine.

How does Paul's teaching help us solve the problem of Christian disunity today? This passage of Scripture doesn't solve every problem, but it does provide the indispensable foundation by showing how limited are our choices. If we follow the pattern of modern

Christianity, we are forced to choose between the two aspects of the faith that are joined together by Paul. Western Protestantism has been forced into a dilemma that Paul rejects. Paul will not have faithfulness to truth without unity in the church, nor will he have unity without commitment to truth. The only way to follow Paul's guidelines is to reject the dilemma outright. The beginning of any Christian unity is to reject unity through negotiation. Unity comes by embracing apostolic truth. Yet embracing truth should not be at the expense of destroying the body of Christ, the church. The answer does not lie in either/or. It lies in both/and.

The solution to the problem of Christian disunity that Paul hints at in I Corinthians is developed more fully in one of his later letters, Ephesians. The Fourth Chapter of Ephesians contains Paul's rich teaching on unity.

> As a prisoner of the Lord, then, I urge you to live a life worthy of the calling you have received. Be completely humble and gentle; be patient, bearing with one another in love. Make every effort to keep the unity of the Spirit through the bond of peace. There is one body and one Spirit — just as you were called to one hope when you were called — one Lord, one faith, one baptism; one God and Father of all, who is over all, through all and in all. (Ephesians 4:1-6 NIV)

Paul makes two kinds of statements in this passage of Scripture, exhortations and factual truths. The exhortations (e.g. be humble) are the goals for which he urges us to strive. The factual statements are those truths which provide the foundation of what he is exhorting us to do. In essence, Paul says we should be united because there is only one church founded by one Lord and indwelt by one Spirit. Let's examine the exhortations and factual statements in this passage more carefully.

Paul's exhortations recognize that it is possible for Christians to be divided. Unlike Corinth, the church in Ephesus didn't have any obvious problems of schism but the problem of division was always lying under the surface. In Chapter 2 verses 11-22 Paul speaks of the wall of partition between Jews and Gentiles that Christ has destroyed. Most churches of the New Testament times consisted of Jews and Gentiles — a problem evident in Galatians — and this ethnic difference always posed a problem for unity. Paul's exhortations to unity then in Chapter Four are not empty. There are two sides to his commands. One is the gentle side and the other is the diligence required to maintain unity. Humility, meekness and patience are the key attitudes that will preserve the unity of the church. Forbearance toward fellow Christians is an essential instrument of unity.

At the same time, diligence to keep unity is essential. When Paul says in v.3 that we should be diligent to maintain the unity of the Spirit, he is teaching that unity is a gift of the Holy Spirit, not something we produce. The phrase *unity of the Spirit* could be translated *the unity that comes from the Spirit*. What the Spirit gives we must work hard at keeping. The way to do this is *through the bond of peace* but not an ordinary peace. Our Lord told us he would give us *his* peace (cf Jn 14:27). The Spirit's peace is Christ's peace through the Holy Spirit. Since Christ is one, his peace also binds together believers into one body. Even if Christians are divided, their divisions are not permanent or irreparable. The bond that Christ's peace produces can overcome all human divisions. The facts of division today might discourage us from believing that Christian unity is ever possible, but Paul would have us rise above our own limitations by looking to a much greater power. Paul begins this section 4:1-6 with the word *therefore* (*then* in the NIV). This transitional word invites us to examine the previous verses which tell us that God is able to do far above what we can ask or think:

> To him who is able to do immeasurably more than all we ask or imagine, according to his power that is at work in us, to him be glory in the church and in Christ Jesus throughout all generations, for ever and ever! Amen. (Eph. 3:20,21 NIV)

Christian unity is not possible within the limitations of human powers, but God is far beyond our limitations. That's why Paul stresses that God *far exceeds* our expectations. Paul's hope was in the power of God, but it is not an abstract power that had no relation to our world and its needs. He speaks of *God's power that is at work in us* which is why he also wants glory *in the church.* Paul's exhortations to unity are based upon the solid confidence that God is working in the church to do what we do not think is possible. All that is required on our part is humility, gentleness and diligence. These virtues are required if unity is to be achieved, but they are also gifts of the Spirit. In short, the unity that we desire is beyond our power. We cannot create unity. All we can do is maintain the unity the Spirit gives. God can create Christian unity because he has already provided the foundation of that unity in the church.

Paul's factual statements begin in verse 4, *there is one body* etc. These statements equally recognize that it is not possible for the church to be divided. Christians may be divided, but the church cannot be. The foundation for our overcoming divisions among Christians is that God has already provided the unity we seek. This is important because Christians often speak of the church as divided as if there were many churches in the world. On a physical level, this is true; there are many churches. Paul obviously knew of churches in many different locations throughout the world and he sometimes uses the term *church* to refer to particular congregations. For example, he wrote to the *churches* of the Galatian region of Asia Minor (cf. Gal 1:2).

Yet in Ephesians Paul says that there is one body of Christ. His statements cannot be casual, off-hand remarks for two reasons. He makes the same point at length in I Corinthians Chapters 12-14. And here in Ephesians 4, Paul couples things that are on the same order of existence. What things are one? *One body, one Spirit, one hope, one Lord, one faith, one baptism, one God and Father of all.* Paul lists seven things here that cannot be divided and sums up the faith by invoking each member of the Trinity. The one Holy Spirit cannot be divided. The one Lord, probably referring to Jesus, cannot be divided. The one God and Father cannot be divided. If God himself cannot be torn apart or divided, what about the remaining four things that also are said to be one. How many hopes does the Christian have? There is but one hope, the blessed hope of Christ's glorious appearing (cf. Tit 2:13). How many faiths are there for the

Christian? Only one. What about baptism? Only one Christian baptism. If these things are true, then it is also true that there is only one body of Christ i.e. one church. The reality of only one church is the foundation to which Paul calls us. We can be unified as Christians because there is only one church. The church of Jesus Christ can no more be divided than God himself can be divided.

Paul's teaching has profound implications for our search for visible unity. The cycle of choosing either truth and division or unity and compromise is broken by Paul's understanding of the church in I Corinthians 1:10-17 and Ephesians 4:1-6. When the scepter of disunity raises its ugly head, we must do two things Paul teaches. First, we must return to the same Gospel that the apostles taught. Paul sought to correct errors by reiterating the truths of the Christian faith. These truths provide us with the objective basis for calling into question all the individual agendas of various parties. Paul called the Corinthians to unity by emphasizing the one indivisible Christ and the baptism he commanded (I Cor 1:13). He calls the Ephesians to unity based on the same Lord and his one church. To embrace apostolic truth means *to embrace the unity of the church that already exists.* The second essential step is to seek humbly the unity that the Spirit gives and reject our own contrived unity. Such will take all the gentleness and meekness we can muster by the Spirit's power. But one way we'll achieve such gentleness is by acknowledging *one Lord, one faith and one baptism.* That acknowledgement should produce within us a willingness to relinquish our own agendas for unity and make sure that we adopt Paul's divinely inspired agenda.

Paul's teaching helps us overcome two tendencies repeated throughout the history of Christianity, reductions and additions. Returning to the Gospel means that these two errors must be avoided. Reductionism is the attempt to make Christianity *less than the fullness of Jesus' teaching and work.* This can happen the way it did in Protestant Liberalism by reducing the content of the Gospel to a few broad guidelines. Liberalism was a Christianity without Christ. It can also happen by reducing the Christian life to accepting Jesus as your personal Savior. Both forms of reductionism are not hypothetical; they both have occurred in twentieth century Christianity. They both betray the Gospel because they do not teach everything that Jesus commanded (cf. Mt 5:18,19; 28:20). The other tendency is additions to the Gospel. Additions are teachings added to the faith that are not consistent with the principles of the Gospel. Additions are not the same as clarifications. Clarifications are doctrinal or creedal statements that explain the Gospel and its implications. They are necessary when the culture in which the Gospel is preached misunderstands it. Catholicism has been one of the primary targets with this criticism in the history of Christianity. As a Protestant Christian, I believed that doctrines of Mary were such additions. They are not the Gospel, I used to say. They are unwarranted additions. The problem of course is how we distinguish between legitimate clarifications of the Gospel and illegitimate additions. But the answer lies already in what we've seen in Ephesians Chapter Four. Just as there is one Lord, one faith and one baptism, so there is one Church. And that one Church is God's chosen instrument to distinguish between legitimate clarifications and illegitimate additions. This is why Paul calls the Church *the pillar and foundation of the truth* (I Tim 3:15). And the Church of history shows how God the Holy Spirit has guided the body of Christ to perform this task through the councils of the ancient Church. The historic Church is not the ultimate basis of the truth. The God who revealed the Gospel is the ultimate foundation of truth. The Church is his servant. It is this one God in the person of Christ who committed the Gospel to the Church. And it was the apostolic founders of the Church (and their cohorts) who wrote down the Gospel in many forms and ways in the New Testament. When there's a question about the content of the Gospel as expressed in Scripture, it is to the Church that we must turn to distinguish between legitimate clarifications and illegitimate additions.

Paul's teaching on the unity of the Church provides some of the most powerful answers to the problem of Christian disunity. They have been there in the New Testament all along, but often we have failed to read and understand carefully the implications of his teaching. We must be satisfied with nothing less than the one Church that Jesus founded (Mt 16: 13-18). It was that Church which Paul and the other apostles worked to establish. At the same time, the Church of Jesus Christ cannot be a church of our own contriving. It must be the way Jesus Christ wants his Church to be. It must be the

Church that Paul speaks of in Ephesians 5:21-33. It must be the Church which Christ loved and for which he gave himself (5:25) and which he sanctified by the cleansing with the washing of the water in word (5:26). It must be the Church he will present to himself glorious without any spot or wrinkle (5:27). This Church is the bride who has adorned herself for the wedding supper of the Lamb (Rev. 19:7). This personal language of marriage and love points back to a kind of unity for which our Lord prayed.

One People with One Heart John 17

No passage in all of Scripture compares to the loveliness and tenderness expressed by our Lord in his high priestly prayer in John Chapter Seventeen. If we can imagine the agony of his experience, we can see the great generosity of his heart as he prayed for his own. Here we see Jesus in intimate communion with the Father as he realizes that his earthly journey nears the end and he is returning to the Father.

Our Lord's high priestly prayer shows us the goal of life, union with God for eternity. His own unity with the Father is the basis of our unity. He asks for the Father to glorify him on earth (Jn 17:1) that he may pass that glory on to his own disciples. And here we see what kind of unity our Lord desires for us. He wants us to experience the kind of glory he had with the Father before the world existed (Jn 17:5). Jesus' disciples were given to him by the Father (Jn 17:2,6) and he has faithfully given them the Father's truth (Jn 17:8). When Jesus prayed for the unity of his followers, he prayed that their unity may be the same as what he and the Father had (*that they may be one just as we are one* 17:11).

Verse 21 gives us a more explicit truth, *that they may be one just as you, Father, are in me and I in you, that they also may be in us*. Not just any unity will do. Only the complete unity that reflects and comes from the Trinity will answer to our Lord's request. The mutual indwelling of the Father and the Son (theologically called *circumincessio*) provides the source of the Church's unity. This is why unity by negotiation is so impotent. All the human contrivances we can conceive will never unify Christians in the manner Jesus prayed for. Only the indwelling fullness of the great Triune

God will accomplish unity. How does that happen? Verse 22 tells us, *I have given them the glory you [Father] gave me that they may be one as we are one.* Unity among Christians comes only by the reception of divine glory that Jesus brought to our world. Recall that John told us that Jesus as the Incarnate Word (*Logos*) was full of grace and truth (Jn 1:14) and that *from his fullness we have all received* (Jn 1:16). That grace, truth and glory that fills his being is now ours through his earthly ministry. As he prays for us, our Lord wishes that same glory to so fill the hearts of his faithful ones that divisions may cease and the divine oneness may fill the Church.

Believing that unity among Christians is possible would be a sham if it depended on human ingenuity and effort. But God can accomplish in moments what human beings never can. The glory of Jesus Christ can fill each and every Christian with such grace, love and truth that he or she will want the kind of unity Christ provides. What is required on our part? Jesus says that we must keep the message (word) which he delivered from the Father (Jn 17:6). That is why commitment to *his* truth is so vital. We must put our personal agendas aside and follow his path. When Jesus prayed, *Holy Father, keep them in your name* (Jn 17:11) and *sanctify them in your truth* (Jn 17:17), he was asking that the truth and character of the Father's person might be the center of our lives. Nothing less will achieve his goal of the union of all God's children in the Father.

Mary: The Sign of Unity?

How can Mary help in promoting Christian unity? Many may feel the weight of disunity among Christians and long for a greater oneness in Christ, but can Mary really give us that greater oneness? Mary has been a source of division between Catholics and Protestants for a long time. What good will focusing on Mary bring? How can Christians be one when the very Marian devotions so precious to Catholics are viewed as idolatrous by Protestants? To human eyes, it seems that almost any other Christian doctrine would be better suited to bring unity than doctrines of Mary. And if we think of Mary just as a set of doctrine, that would be true. But Mary is more than a set of doctrines. Mary is a person. She lived her life on this earth as the mother of our Lord with her own character, mind, and idiosyncracies. These things are true regardless of what we believe about her. Mary is what she is apart from our beliefs. There is one unmistakable fact that we must remember about the real Mary, the Son of God lived in her womb for nine months. This is how Mary can be an instrument of unity. She united the Logos, the second person of the Trinity, with his human nature in her own body. Mary united more than any human being has ever united. She united God and man in the small confines of her own womb. Ponder this amazing reality. In Mary's womb, heaven and earth were joined, not as two separate realities, but perfectly united in the one person of the Son of God. No wonder it says that "Mary treasured all these things and pondered them in her heart." (Lk 2:19). It is a reality beyond words. Mary was the instrument of unity for the body of Jesus Christ and this is why Mary has long been thought of as mother of the Church. The Church is the body of Christ and Mary was the mother of Christ's body, both physically and mystically. We've seen in the biblical texts discussed in this chapter that Jesus Christ is the key to unity among Christians. But the one Savior Jesus Christ would not be what he is — the perfect God-man — without Mary's being the means of uniting his divine and human natures in one person.

Mary's example of obedience and discipleship also form the foundation of unity. Mary gave herself unreservedly to Jesus her Son. Every Christian wants to be an obedient discipleship of our Lord and needs examples of obedience to do so. Mary was filled with grace and this allowed her to listen to the commands of her God without delay. Mary was on earth what every Christian will become in heaven, filled with grace. Obedience means a readiness to say YES to God, a spirit of humility that says *fiat*. We've seen in this chapter that unity cannot be achieved through negotiation. It must come through obedience to the apostolic teaching given by Jesus to Paul and the other apostles. Without a willing spirit, we can never achieve God's desire for unity. Mary's life of obedience and discipleship calls us to unity with God through obedience.

How can Mary help Christians find a greater unity among themselves? Mary has been a source of disagreements between Catholics and Protestants for a long time. Of all the truths Christians believe, Mary seems to be the least likely of all to help with the problem of unity. But we must recall the kind of unity we should seek. If we were looking for unity through negotiation where each side gives up something for the sake of a common faith, then Mary would indeed be a stumbling block to unity. Yet the unity we seek is not human but divine. Its source is the divine life of Christ the Redeemer. It is that unity for which he prayed when he said, "Father, that they might be one." This kind of unity doesn't come from each group of Christians giving up some belief or practice for the sake of unity; it comes from each individual or group submitting to the authority of Christ and from the work of the Holy Spirit bringing oneness where it is humanly impossible. Like salvation itself, Christian unity is not within the grasp of human power. All we can do is open ourselves up to the ministry of the Spirit to produce the unity that is impossible through negotiation.

It is because Mary has been such a stumbling block for Christians that a fuller embracing of her person and role will achieve a greater unity than we might expect. If we view Mary apart from Jesus, then Mary cannot help us. Yet she was never meant to be seen apart from her Son. Just as the Magi found Jesus "with his mother" (Mt 2:11), so we find Mary involved with her divine Son, cooperating in his work and plan.

We cannot solve the problem of how to be one in Christ. Not by negotiation, not by one or the other side caving in. But God can solve our problems. God specializes in the impossible, just as he once said to Mary (Lk 1:37). If the Holy Spirit can create within the womb of the Virgin Mary a new entity — the unique God-man — then he surely can bring together Christians divided by history, suspicion and misinformation. Perhaps it's time for us to stop trying to be unified and let God do what we have failed to do. No one can see precisely how this will happen, but we know it won't happen without embracing the fullness of salvation in Christ himself. In the next chapter, we will see how the message of salvation in the Old Testament leads to one people of God in the Messiah.

CHAPTER FOUR

THE HOPE OF SALVATION IN MARY'S WORLD

Mary was a young Jewish woman who was probably not over sixteen years of age when Gabriel appeared to her. Her *bat-mitzvah* at age twelve or thirteen allowed Mary to become an adult woman and assume all the responsibilities laid upon her by the commands of the Old Testament Scriptures (*Torah*). It is not unusual that she was engaged at this age since Jewish girls could be married at any time after their *bat-mitzvah*. In most ways, Mary probably lived a normal and uneventful life, indistinguishable from those her own age. Her life was to change dramatically very soon in ways she never expected. Yet we will not be able to understand Mary's extraordinary person unless we know the history, culture and surroundings of her daily life. At the heart of her life was the *Torah*, those instructions and hopes that were expressed in the Old Testament Scriptures. Let's recast Mary's world by looking to the same Scriptures she must have learned as a child.

The following three chapters (4,5,6) are not about Mary directly but they do provide the indispendable foundation to understand Mary as she is discussed in the last two chapters (7,8). One reason so many misunderstandings about Mary prevail is that so few Christians understand the plan of salvation anticipated in the Old Testament. In this chapter, we will see some of the prominent themes of salvation that find fulfillment in the life of our Savior and of his mother. The better we grasp these Old Testament themes, the better we will see how necessary Mary is to God's plan of salvation.

Salvation as God's Presence

Let's begin with a basic question. *What is salvation? What does it mean to be saved?* As an evangelical Christian for many years, I thought the answer to that question was straightforward. Salvation was accepting Jesus Christ as my personal Savior. Doesn't Romans 10: 9 say, "if you confess with your mouth Jesus as Lord and believe in your heart that God raised him from the dead, you will be saved?" At its simplest level, it is true that accepting Christ as one's personal Savior is the heart of salvation. But there is so much more in the Bible. When I began studying theology formally and then later teaching in a Protestant seminary, I discovered that the apparently simple statement of Romans 10:9 contains a wealth of hopes and promises that most Christians never see. Marriage is a perfect analogy. When I said, "I do" on 21 December 1974, I said two simple words, but little did I realize then that those words contained a whole lifetime of understanding. So too, accepting Christ is the foundation of our salvation, but there's so much more in the Bible. If we want more than a minimal Jesus, we must understand the Scriptures which Mary learned as a child and which later she taught her own child Jesus.

One word sums up salvation in the Old Testament — Covenant. As a Presbyterian biblical scholar, I spent several years emphasizing the truths of the covenant as they are taught in Scripture. The Reformed faith was blessed with an abundance of attention to the concept of the covenant. And rightly so! Covenant is the one word in the Bible that summarizes everything we believe and live as Christians. This is why Jesus spoke those unforgettable words on the night of his passion, "this cup is the new covenant in my blood." (Lk 22:20). What does *covenant* mean? The Bible nowhere gives a dictionary definition and yet we can infer its meaning through the repeated phrases used in the Old Testament. The Lord revealed himself to Abraham at the outset of salvation history so that he might become the father of many nations (Gen 12:2; 17:5). In Genesis 17, God binds Abraham to himself by using a covenant:

> I am God Almighty; walk before me and be blameless.
> I will confirm my covenant between me and you and
> will greatly increase your numbers. (17:2)

> I will establish my covenant as an everlasting covenant
> between me and you and your descendants after you for
> the generations to come, to be your God and the God of
> your descendants after you. (17:7)

The wording of 17:7 gives us the essence of the covenant that God offers Abraham and us, "to be your God and the God of your descendants after you." Salvation is more than acceptance with God in a strictly legal sense. Salvation is to have a living relationship with God. To have a relationship is to live together, to work together, to spend life together. And our God is far more personal than we are. He wants us to live with him in his family. The relationship via covenant of Gen 17:7 was implied already in what God told Abraham in Gen 15:1, "Don't be afraid Abram. I am your shield and very great reward." Abraham's joy and salvation was by having God as his own God, to relate to God as his chief possession.

The covenant as a relationship is so important in the Old Testament that it is repeated again and again, but it is especially noteworthy when the biblical writers teach it at crucial junctures in Israel's history. One such time was in Jeremiah's day when Judah was about to be hauled off to exile in Babylon. In Jeremiah Chapter 30-33 (what scholars call the Book of Comfort), the renewal of the covenant is promised in which all God's people will be restored to that relationship with Yahweh:

> I am with you and will save you, declares the Lord.
> (30:11)

> So you will be my people and I will be your God. (30:22)

> At that time, declares the Lord, I will be the God of all
> the clans of Israel, and they will be my people. (31:1)

> I have loved you with an everlasting love. I have drawn
> you with loving kindness. (31:3)
>
> They will be my people and I will be their God. (32:38)

At a time when God's people needed reassurance, God tells them
that he has not forgotten them and that his presence will save them
(see 30:11). This is the heart of the new covenant promised in Jer
31:31-33:

> The time is coming when I will make a new covenant
> with the house of Israel and with the house of Judah. It
> will not be like the covenant I made with their forefa-
> thers when I took them out of Egypt because they broke
> my covenant though I was husband to them ... this is the
> covenant I will make with the house of Israel after that
> time, declares the Lord. I will put my law in their minds
> and write it on their hearts. I will be their God and they
> will be my people.

The new covenant is both similiar and dissimiliar to the old one.
Jeremiah's words stress how different they are because the new
covenant will not be broken as the old one was. Yet the heart of
both the old and the new covenants is the same, *I will be their God
and they will be my people.* Both sides of this relationship are
vital. All of us know how human relationships can be one-sided,
one person loving more than the other. The covenant that God
made with ancient Israel was also one-sided. Yahweh loved Israel
and did everything for his people, but Israel repeatedly turned away
from Yahweh (cf. Is. 5:1ff). The new covenant promises God's
people will now respond to God as He has come to them — with
complete fidelity. This covenant under the Messiah promises a
new intimacy with God that will win the hearts of a wayward
people. How is that intimacy possible?

Salvation is the presence of God from beginning to end in the
Bible. Salvation is knowing God by God coming to know us. The
intimacy promised in the new covenant was already prepared in

the old. The greatest salvation event in the old covenant was the Exodus from Egypt. From that time on, God's deliverance of his people from the hand of Pharoah became the great sign of God's future salvation through the Messiah. This is why the words of Hosea 11:1 could be used to speak of both past and future, "When Israel was a child, I loved him, and out of Egypt I called my son." This text spoke of the historical Exodus but also of Jesus' return from Egypt after Herod's persecutions (cf. Mt 2:15). The Exodus was more than a relocation program for the Jews. It was God's way of bringing his people to himself.

> You yourselves have seen what I did to Egypt, and how I carried you on eagles' wings and brought you to myself. (Ex 19:4).

In one verse we have a summary of salvation itself. God brought harsh judgment on Egypt that meant the salvation of his people. He provided a glorious salvation that was far beyond their wildest dreams ("I carried you on eagles' wings"). But the greatest of all was the final, personal union ("I brought you to myself"). What would salvation be if it were only miracles to inspire awe or a new home for Israel? No, salvation is so much more, nothing less than union with God himself. "I will be your God and you will be my people."

So, it's not surprising to find the prophets proclaiming a heightened and renewed presence of God among his people in the Messianic age. Sometimes this promise is in very general terms such as *the Lord will be with you*. Other times it's very specific and concrete, "The Lord will suddenly come to his temple." (Mal 3:1). Sometimes it's implied in the language used in a text like Haggai 2:5 — ("I am with you, says the Lord. And this is the covenant I made with you when you departed Egypt — My Spirit is standing in your midst.") — where the word *standing* may be an allusion to the pillar of fire. Other times the imagery of the Exodus is used to evoke the remembrance of God's presence such as Zech 2:5 "I myself will be a wall of fire around it [Jerusalem] and I will be its glory within". These and many more are all ways in which the prophets proclaim salvation as God's presence.

However, this promise of divine presence takes its most scandalous form when it speaks of God coming as a child:

> Therefore, the Lord will give you a sign. A virgin will conceive and will give birth to a son whose name will be called Immanuel. (Is 7:14)

This text, quoted by Matthew in 1:23 and immortalized in Handel's *Messiah*, could not have left any doubt in the minds of its original hearers. The Hebrew words *Immanu with us* and *El God* would have rung out with the central message of salvation and the covenant — God is finally here for good. The Jews of Jesus' day didn't miss the message. The birth of Jesus was nothing less than the Messianic age's final arrival. It was a *sign* — the biblical term always means an object that points to something greater than itself —— for all to know that God was now on earth with his covenant people. Just as God had once "come down to rescue them from the hand of the Egyptians" (Ex 3:8), so he had come down again for the final Exodus from bondage.

The birth narrative in Luke's Gospel is replete with this theme of salvation as God's final gift of his presence. Though physically in the New Testament, Luke Chapters 1 & 2 are really Old Testament hopes come to fulfillment. When a startled Zechariah, the father-to-be of John the Baptist, trembles before the angel Gabriel, the messenger of God reminds the old man, "I stand in the presence of God." (Luke 1:19) And when the priest becomes a father beyond his wildest dreams, he exclaims, "Praise be the Lord, the God of Israel, because he has come and has redeemed his people" (Lk 1:68). This *God-coming-to-his-people* is in fact the major theme of Zechariah's song in Luke 1:67-79:

> He raised up a horn of salvation for us in the house of David his servant (1:69)

> To show mercy to our fathers and to remember his holy covenant (1:72)

And you, my child, will be called a prophet of the Most
High for you will go on before the Lord to prepare the
way for him. (1:76)

because of the tender mercies of our God, by which the
rising sun will come to us from heaven. (1:78)

This selection of verses from Zechariah's song shows a deep ap-
prehension of the mercy of God that permeates the covenant promises. Zechariah sees in his son, John, the fulfillment not only of his
own personal life but the hope of Israel expressed throughout the
Old Testament.

Luke 1:78 is especially powerful but likely to be overlooked.
The first phrase ("because of the tender mercies of our God")
means that the saving power of God's presence all flows from the
same source, the inexhaustible mercy of God's heart. The second
phrase ("the rising sun will come to us from heaven") tells what
the divine mercy does, what it accomplishes. It brings us the
Messiah himself rising with healing in his wings. The above translation, while literal, obscures its powerful meaning. The Greek
word *anatole* indeed means *rising sun* but the word was used in
Greek translations of Zech 3:8 for the Hebrew *tsemach*, usually
translated *branch*. *Tsemach* was a technical term used by the prophets Isaiah (4:2), Jeremiah (23:5) and Zechariah to speak of the
Messiah as rising over Israel to bring light to God's people. In
Luke 1:78, the verb translated *come* is really *episkeptomai* meaning *to overlook, to watch over, to overshadow*. So, the verse could
be paraphrase as follows:

All this will happen because of the constant acts of mercy
that flow from our God. By these acts of mercy the Rising Light of God from on high will come over us and
protect us.

Zechariah the priest may be drawing on the Old Testament prophet
whose name he bears to proclaim the blessings of the Messiah as
the new light to Israel and the world. In short, Zechariah's song of

praise extolls the truth: God is finally here for good and his presence *is* our salvation.

All these promises belonged to Mary as a daughter of the covenant, and we know that she embraced them with a heart full of faith. When Mary heard the praises of her elderly cousin, Elizabeth, she broke forth in praise of the God of Abraham and sung of his covenant faithfulness:

> *He has helped his servant Israel by remembering his mercies just as he told our fathers, to Abraham and his seed forever.* (Lk 1:54,55)

Like all pious Jews in that day, Mary was waiting for *the consolation of Israel* (Lk 2:25). She realized that she was a daughter of Sarah and that God had not abandoned his people. She spent years as a child nurturing her faith on the covenant promises of the Old Testament. She knew God would send a Messiah for Israel, but she had no idea that God's plan of redemption would involve her directly.

Miraculous Births in Salvation

The God who sends his presence in a specific, local manner is also the God of the miraculous. Throughout the Old Testament we find a theme of miraculous birth follows Israel's progress to the Messianic age. We saw in Chapter One how Mary's *Magnificat* was modeled on Hanna's song of praise for the birth of Samuel. It is no accident that the birth of the Messiah was a miraculous event. That pattern reaches back to the very beginning of salvation of history — back to Abraham and Sarah.

The story of Abraham and Sarah in Genesis Chapter Twelve begins God's call of a particular people out of the world. We already saw how the relationship between God and Abraham was framed as a covenant, a binding relatinship in which God gave his own presence to Abraham and expected Abraham's total allegiance (Gen 17:1). The Lord who appeared to Abraham is also the author of life, and therefore, an essential part of salvation is fruitfulness.

God's love always bears fruit. And the promise of having a multitude of descendants was an essential part of Abraham's salvation (see Gen 17:2-7). If these things are true, why did God wait until Abraham and Sarah were too old to have children to reveal Himself to them?

Salvation is from the Lord, Yahweh. That is the message of Abraham's and Sarah's lives. The child of promise born to them did not come during the natural childbearing years. And so Genesis Chapter Eighteen emphasizes how Yahweh challenged Abraham and Sarah to believe his promise of the miraculous birth of Isaac. Genesis 18:14 is the key verse, "is anything too difficult for the Lord?" These words echo again in the account of the announcement of Jesus' birth when Gabriel says to Mary, "for nothing is impossible with God." (Lk 1:37). The Hebrew word in Genesis 18:14 that is often translated *difficult* or *hard* has the connotation of *wonder* or *awe-inspiring*. So, it could be translated, "Is anything so wonderful, so unbelievable that the Lord can't do it?" The birth of Isaac gave a resounding answer to that question. God can do anything he needs to save his people. And not only can he do it; he specializes in the miraculous so his people will know that salvation isn't accomplished by human power.

The theme of miraculous birth permeates the Old Testament and plays directly into the hope of the Messiah in Isaiah 7:14:

> The Lord himself will give you a sign: the virgin will be with child and will give birth to a son, and will call him Immanuel.

This theme explains two important facts about the Incarnation. It explains why Luke chose to tell us so much about the birth of John the Baptist, and why Jesus was born of a virgin. John the Baptist was born to an old couple, Zechariah and Elizabeth, because such an unexpected birth was itself a sign that salvation must be on the way. But it also explains why Jesus was *not* just born to an old couple. Since this child was God with us (*Immanuel*), it would not do to have a birth like others, wondrous though they were. This birth had to be totally unique while building on the theme of the unusual births to Sarah, to Hanna, and to Elizabeth. Salvation is experiencing the very presence of God, but it is utterly astounding that such a presence should come bodily, physically and through a simple woman. That God should come in human form as a man is the greatest scandal the world has ever known. This is the very reason why Christianity is such a stumbling block to many. The Incarnation proclaims that God is here with us, indeed that God is one of us. Human beings find that impossible to believe. And that is why the Eucharist is so hard, so difficult to believe. It is the continuation of the Incarnation. Jesus is still with us in his body and blood. Salvation is God's presence, eaten but never consumed.

Salvation for the World: A Catholic People

Another theme that fills the story of Jesus' birth in the Gospel of Luke tells of salvation for all the world. One of the reasons that early Christians were persecuted in the Roman world comes from the name *Catholic*, from the Greek word *katholikos* meaning universal. As long as religions were local and did not intrude into others' territories, the Roman government had a hands-off attitude toward the diversity of religions under their power. But the Christian church claimed to be universal, for all men and nations, in short, to be catholic. That claim to universality was a threat to the pluralism of antiquity. But early Christians had no choice for the dictates of their own faith required proclamation of salvation for all the world. That truth is already expressed in Jesus' birth but is rooted in the Old Testament.

The seed of Old Testament universality grows in the bosom of Abraham to whom God said, "You will be a father of many nations" (Gen 17:3). And Paul explains this promise by saying that Abraham knew he would inherit the world (Rom 4:13). His was not a plan to redeem one nation only, nor even a collection of peoples scattered throughout the earth. No, the only plan befitting Yahweh's sovereign universality was salvation for all that were in Adam. "As in Adam all died, so in Christ will all be made alive" (I Co. 15:22).

The prophets of Israel detailed the world-wide scope of the Messiah's work in a variety of pictures drawn in the colors of ancient life. Isaiah painted the portrait of Yahweh's mountain where all the nations of the earth come:

> In the last days, the mountain of the Lord's temple will
> be established as chief among the mountains; it will be
> raised above the hills, and all nations will stream to it.
> (Is 2:2).

Here the flood of salvation seekers flows to Mt. Zion in search of
God himself. The nations see the beauty and grace of God, and
are drawn to his mercy. What will they find when they arrived at
Mt. Zion?

> He will teach us his ways that we may walk in his paths
> ... they will beat their swords into plowshares and their
> spears into pruning hooks. Nation will not take up sword
> against nation nor will they learn war anymore. (Is 2:3,4)

The Messiah's reign brings what he himself is i.e. the Prince of
Peace (Is 9:6). Nation arrayed against nation dissolves into work-
ers standing side by side in the new Mt. Zion where Yahweh's peace,
his total *Shalom*, reigns supreme. In Isaiah's portrait of the final
days, the nations will come when the banner of return is hoisted
high (Is 11:12) and when the former enemies of Israel are counted
among God's people.

> In that day there will be an altar to the Lord in the heart
> of Egypt (Is 19:19)

> The Lord will make himself known to the Egyptians,
> and in that day they will acknowledge the Lord. (Is 19:21)

> In that day Israel will be a third, along with Egypt and
> Assyria, a blessing on the earth. The Lord Almighty
> will bless them, saying, "Blessed be Egypt my people,
> and Assyria my handiwork, and Israel my inheritance.
> (Is 19:24,24)

All the barriers that human beings erect to fence off others from
their lives will be demolished by the divine mercy that extends to
all inhabitants of the globe. How could the church be anything but

Catholic with this promise of nation after nation streaming to the living waters of salvation (cf. Is 12:3).

What will these people groups do, once they have arrived at the place of God's redemption? They will sit down to a banquet where they will feast on the finest of God's saving food:

> On this mountain, the Lord Almighty will prepare a feast of rich food for all peoples, a banquet of aged wine — the best of meats and finest of wines. On this mountain, he will destroy the shroud that enfolds all peoples, the sheet that covers the nations; he will swallow up death forever. The Sovereign Lord will wipe away the tears from all faces; he will remove the disgrace of his people from all the earth. (Is 25:6-8)

These texts are a small sampling of the prophetic promise of a reunited people of God in the age of the Messiah. The northern kingdom of Israel and the southern kingdom of Judah are to be reunited as Israel becomes the place of pilgrimmage for all the pagan nations of the world.

The hope of a universal (catholic) salvation finds similar expression in the Psalms of ancient Israel. The Psalms are another manifestation of the great variety God used to convey his saving truths. They formed an essential part of synagogue worship that Mary must have known as a little girl, and they continued to shape the worship of the new covenant people of God (i.e. the church). God spoke through the praises of his people as much as he did through the prophets. This praisebook of Israel has served the church since its inception in the weekly liturgy, in the divine office of the monasteries, in the preaching of the great orators, and in the private reflections of God's faithful ones.

The Psalms express the reality of God's universal work of salvation by calling on the nations to join Israel in worship of the true God:

> Shout for joy, all the earth
> Serve the Lord with gladness
> Come before Him with joyful songs
> (Ps. 100:1)

In all likelihood, Mary grew up knowing and singing the Psalms. If she did, she could not have failed to see the theme of Yahweh's universal salvation. When Psalm 96 urged God's people to proclaim his glory among the nations, Mary must have known that she, as one of God's chosen daughters, would also be an instrument in bringing divine mercy to others. When Mary meditated on the words of Psalm 2 and Psalm 110, she would have longed for the day when the One who sat at Yahweh's right hand would bring every nation under his rule. Knowing Psalm 19 said "heavens declare the glory of God," she would have felt an obligation to join the celestial trumpets in bringing the knowledge of God to everyone everywhere.

Mary and the Hope of Israel

Mary grew up in a world filled with hope because Israel's hope had become hers through the instruction and worship of her people. She hoped for the salvation of her people, the Jews, and this perhaps had certain political dimensions to it. But Mary knew that the salvation which God would bring far transcended any particular political arrangement. Her hope rested on the promise of God himself coming to dwell among his people. Only Yahweh's final and permanent presence would satisfy all the special promises of the Hebrew Scriptures that shaped Mary's hope. Those particular promises spoke of a Redeemer who would extend his rule from sea to sea. She knew that salvation was intended for all peoples and could not be limited to Jews alone. What she didn't know, or could ever guess, was how God would fulfill this promise, or what woman he would choose to bring the Redeemer into the world.

Given what we have seen about Mary's faith and obedience, it is reasonable to believe that she longed for the day when God's people would no longer be torn by internal strife or external assaults. She grew up in a remote corner of the Roman Empire and could feel every day the threats of foreign power on her native soil. She could also see the Jews divided and torn into various sects — Pharisees, Saducees, Essenes, Zealots — and she probably saw how none of this world reflected the beautiful promises of the Old Testament. She had set her hopes on something higher, on a day when God himself would come to reunite his people and all his elect into the one people of God. But how would the Lord do this? Mary could only guess.

CHAPTER FIVE

CHRIST THE ONLY SAVIOR

The campfire glowed with its characteristic warmth as Joseph and Mary prepared to sleep. Tomorrow night they would be in Bethlehem. Mary knew her time was near. Those nine months had given her a lot of time to reflect on Gabriel's words. And the hopes of her Jewish faith that had shaped her heart from childhood left her in no doubt about one thing: the Son she was soon to bear was Israel's only hope. She had long meditated on the complex and nuanced pictures of the Messiah spread across the pages of the Hebrew Bible. Prophet, priest, king, servant, branch of David, heir of Abraham, light of the Gentiles, rod of Jesse, the scepter from Judah. The list was inexhaustible. And some had even predicted two Messiahs because the Messianic portraits of the Old Testament were so varied, and some thought, contradictory. But Mary knew better. She alone would bear the world's only Redeemer. And all the images of the Scriptures would be true in him. There could be only one Redeemer because there was only one God, and God had to be the Redeemer, or the world would not be redeemed. So Mary waited with a heart mixed with humility and joy, joy because God's Son was also her Son, and humility because more than ever before, she knew she didn't deserve this privilege.

For many years I didn't understand the relationship that Jesus and Mary have. I thought that if we honored and worshipped Jesus, it would imply no honoring of Mary. Honoring Mary detracted from Jesus' glory, I thought. Even after I was strongly attracted to many aspects of Catholicism, I still found myself repelled by what I considered Marian excesses among Catholics. And those excesses do exist in Marian piety. But I also discovered something else quite surprising. My negative reactions to Catholic piety obscured my ability to see the beauty of the relationship between Jesus our Lord and Mary his mother. All that the Catholic Church teaches officially about Mary is based on the total uniqueness of her Son as our Redeemer. Let's explore how Christ is both Mary's Savior and ours.

Chapter Four showed us how God would come in the flesh to save his people by bringing them the fullness of his presence. This background alone demands that there be only one Savior of the human race. No wonder that the New Testament declares, "there is no other name given under heaven by which we can be saved" other than that of Jesus Christ (Acts 4:12) and that "there is one mediator between God and man, the man Christ Jesus." (1 Tim 2:5). Salvation in and through Jesus Christ means that we are united with Christ in his death and resurrection.

Salvation is Union with Christ

Fridays are special days for Christians because one Friday long ago a man hung on a cross outside Jerusalem. This man and his cross are our salvation. But the fact of Jesus' death on the cross alone does not save us. Somehow we have to be connected to his death. We have to be united to it. How does this union happen?

The New Testament expresses salvation in many ways. It speaks of being justified, being sanctified, being born again, being adopted, being given new life, being made a new creation, etc. This diversity of expression can be summarized under the phrase *union with Christ* because no matter how it is said, all these means of expression are ways of saying that we are saved through a relationship with Jesus Christ. We are connected with that man and his cross over the aeons of time. Two of the apostles who wrote in the New Testament have union with Christ at the center of their teachings, John and Paul. Let's take John first.

Think back on the last night of Jesus' life on earth before his death on the cross. As John tells the story, Jesus gave a long speech to his disciples/apostles in John Chapters 14-16. On this occasion,

Thomas is doubtful when Jesus says that they [i.e. the apostles] know the way, "how can we know the way?" Thomas asks. Jesus takes the occasion to probe a little more deeply into Thomas' question by affirming, "I am the way, the truth, and the life. No one comes to the Father except through me" (Jn 14:6). Our Lord here does not content himself with saying that he knows the way or even that he is the way. He goes beyond Thomas' question to say that he is everything we need to find our way to the Father. But Jesus' use of *I am* recalls those earlier occasions when he said similar things: "I am the bread of life" (Jn 6:35), "I am the light of the world" (Jn 8:12), "I am the resurrection and the life" (Jn 11:25). The phrase *I am* becomes doubly significant when Jesus uses it to claim equality with God in Jn 8:58, "truly, truly I tell you, before Abraham was, I am." This text is probably an illusion to the famous passage in Exodus where God reveals his character to Moses through the words, "I am what I am" (Ex 3:14). The name Yahweh seems to be derived from or at least related to the verb *to be* in Hebrew, and so Jesus is making himself equal to Israel's God, Yahweh.

All these expressions in John's presentation of Jesus' life are ways of affirming Jesus as the sole revealer of God the Father and the only Savior of the human race. So, when Jesus says that he is the way, the truth and the life, he teaches that he will be the only path to eternal life. How do we become connected to Jesus? How are we united with Jesus? In John's Gospel, Jesus uses various metaphors, but one of the most important is that of the vine. In John Chapter 15, Jesus says, "I am the vine and you are the branches." This metaphor indicates that we as Jesus' disciples will not find any life except through abiding in him. Jesus is teaching that only by the mutual indwelling of him in us and we in him can we have his life and continue his ministry. This is yet another way of saying that salvation comes through being united to Christ. Apart from Christ we can do nothing (Jn 15:5). Another important metaphor is bread, but in this case the bread turns out to be more than a metaphor. When Jesus says in John 6:35, "I am the bread of life," he goes on to explain himself in 6:51, "if anyone eats of this bread, he will live forever, and the bread that I give is my flesh for the life of the world." These words are not bare metaphors or comparisons. Jesus is *like* a vine in which we must abide as branches (Jn

15:1). Jesus is *like* a door through which we must go to find salvation (Jn 10:9). But Jesus is not just like bread. His flesh is that which he says we must eat in order to find eternal life (Jn 6:53). This eating unites us to him and we receive life from his life.

Paul's teaching on how we are united with Christ is much richer than most Christians imagine. Most concentrate their attention on faith as the sole instrument of salvation. And faith is the bedrock of our relationship with Christ, but faith is never alone in uniting us to him. Paul stresses that faith is connected to the sacraments, which is why he says in Galatians 3:26,27:

> For you are all children of God through faith in Christ Jesus. As many of you as have been baptized into Christ have been clothed with Christ.

Paul stresses that faith is linked to baptism which in turn places us *in Christ*. The imagery of clothing is the apostle's way of saying that we are united to Christ. And the two means by which that act of clothing takes place is faith and baptism. Now it's not as if these are two distinct acts that compete with one another or are completely separate. Faith is the inner invisible element; baptism is the outward.

Paul develops the relationship of faith and baptism more fully in Romans Chapters Five and Six. Paul teaches that we are saved by faith in Romans 5:1, "So, having been justified from faith, we have peace with God through our Lord Jesus Christ." Paul's every word is important. The peace of Christ comes from having his righteousness ("being justified"). When we are clean from sin, we are happy and at peace. How do we obtain Christ's righteousness? "Through faith", says Paul. We can't have righteousness on our own power, by our own works. Righteousness is something we receive. How do we receive it? Paul explains in Chapter Six that it comes through being united to Jesus' death and resurrection, "Don't you know that as many of us as were baptized into Christ Jesus, we were baptized into his death?" (Rom 6:3). The death to sin that we experience in baptism makes us alive to Christ's resurrected life, "as Christ was raised from the dead through the Father's glory, so we too can walk in newness of life." (Rom 6:4). The newness of life means having the righteousness of Christ in us. Baptism is our death to sin that brings justification, "The one who has died has been justified from sin." (Rom 6:7).

In both Galatians and in Romans, Paul is teaching that salvation comes through being united with Christ. That union makes us children of God. The beginning of that union comes through baptism, and coming to baptism is an act of faith because we don't do anything in baptism; we simply receive Christ's righteousness. His righteousness cleans away our sin and gives us peace with God, the main reason why Paul rhetorically asks,"how can we who died to sin still live in it?"(Rom 6:1). Every Christian must live according to the newness of life that has been implanted through baptism.

Now a simple question. Why do John and Paul both emphasize this union with Christ? Why do they not dwell on the Father, or the Holy Spirit more often? The Father plays a prominent role in Jesus' words in John's Gospel. And Paul certainly emphasizes the Father as the one from whom "every fatherhood in heaven and on earth is called." (Eph 3:14). The Holy Spirit is the Paraclete, the Comforter, in John's Gospel (Jn 14:16, 26;16:7). And Paul's doctrine of the Holy Spirit is certainly central to his teaching (see I Co Chap.12-14). But still, there's a greater emphasis on union with Christ in John's Gospel and Letters. And Paul's teaching emphasizes Christ as the central figure in salvation. Why is Christ so central to these apostles' teachings? This simple question demands a simple answer, but sometimes simple answers can be deceiving.

The simple answer is that Christ alone is the Redeemer of the world. Neither the Father nor the Holy Spirit died on the cross or was raised from the dead. And Christ's death was the single most important saving event in history. His death alone paid for our sins. His resurrection vindicated his saving mission showing him to be truly God. But it also gave us new life, eternal life that comes from the Father. Now if only one member of the Trinity was made a man, died and was raised from the dead, then certainly no human creature died or was raised from the dead for our sins. Christ alone did these things.

Yet Christ is never alone. As we saw in chapter two, Jesus alone hung on the cross but Jesus was not alone. And Jesus alone was raised from the dead but Jesus was not alone. He alone ascended into heaven but he was not alone when he did so. When he died on Calvary's hill, there were four who loved him (Jn 19:25). And then there was the soldier who professed his faith (Mk 15:39). When Christ was raised from the dead, the women met him at the tomb (Mt 28:1; Mk 16:1; Lk 24:1ff; Jn 20:1ff). When Jesus ascended into heaven, the apostles were there (see Acts 1:8-11). All these disciples of the Lord were more than bystanders or witnesses. They also received what they witnessed. They experienced his cross, his resurrection and his ascension. And we experience them too. In God's plan, what Jesus experienced, we experience with him. We saw how we died with Christ through baptism (Rom 6:3). Paul also says that "he [the Father] made us *alive together* with Christ and *raised us up* and *seated us with* him in the heavenly realms in Christ Jesus." (Eph 2:5,6). We were united to Jesus' saving work in its very accomplishment.

This union with Christ is the foundation for understanding Mary's place and ours. She is the first of the redeemed. Not in the temporal sense, but in the pre-eminence of her place among the redeemed. She is united with him more deeply than we can imagine. Yet it is the same union we have with Christ our Savior. Jesus Christ is Mary's Savior and ours. We are not saved by our own works of the law, and neither was Mary. She and we are saved by being united with Christ. But Mary's union with her Son is effected differently than ours. Normally, we begin to receive Christ's grace at our baptism. Mary received grace at the first moment of her conception in her mother's womb — a subject we will look at more closely in Chapter Seven. This means that she was redeemed from sin before she was old enough to contract or commit sin. It was a preservative salvation. But both Mary's righteousness and ours flows from union with Christ her Son.

Adam-Christ Parallelism
(Rom. 5:12-21 & I Cor 15:21-22, 45-46)

Why does Paul's teaching emphasize that salvation is union with Christ? One reason is that Paul sees Jesus Christ as the covenant head of the new humanity. Paul develops this idea in a parallelism in which both Adam and Christ are the covenant representatives of their respective peoples. Both acted as representatives for all who are in the covenant. Each one's action affected all under his leadership.

In Adam's case, sin brought death; in Christ's action, righteousness brings life. Adam voluntarily plunged himself and his progeny into sin; Christ voluntarily lifted us up from that same sin. Adam suffered because of his own sin; Christ suffered because of our sins. The effects of Adam's sin are precisely those that Christ the Savior came to repair. Consider the effects of sin. There is the loss of personal integration. The mind, will and emotions no longer cooperate with one another so that people often feel disoriented and listless. There is the disruption of relationships with other people, disunity among the human family. The rancor, hatred, dissension and outright slaughter of whole peoples that have characterized human history witness abundantly to the truth that sin divides people. This is even reflected in our daily language when we speak of different races. In biblical thought, there are no separate races; there is only one human race which manifests itself in different peoples. The disunity of the human family that the fall into sin inaugurated is repaired by the saving work of Jesus Christ.

All this disruption and disunity among human beings is but a meager reflection of the disruption every human being has with God. We are lost by our very sinful nature inherited from Adam. Look at effects of Adam's sin in Romans 5:12-21:

> Death reigned over even those who did not sin in the likeness of Adam's transgressions. (5:14)

> Many died through the transgressions of the one [Adam]. (5:15)

> Judgment from the one resulted in condemnation. (5:16)

And what Adam brought us didn't come from just any sin he happened to commit. It was *that first sin* into which he and Eve fell that plunged humanity into alienation from God. Paul stresses this in Romans 5:18a, "Therefore, through the one transgression we have all men receiving condemnation." No wonder Paul's teaching has Christ at the center. With the moral chaos of Adam's sin, how could anyone redeem humanity except the infinite God-man?

What did Christ's redemption bring? Paul leaves no room for doubt. Christ undid all that Adam did. Christ untied the knot of Adam's transgression, so to speak, and freed those bound by Adam's act of rebellion. Look how Paul balances all his statements about Adam with corresponding ones about Christ:

> Much more God's grace and his gift in grace abounded to many through the one man Jesus Christ. (5:15)

> The free gift resulted from many transgressions resulting in righteousness. (5:16)

> The one righteous act resulted in justification of life for all. (5:18)

Now we can see why Jesus Christ is so central for Paul's teaching. Christ is the only one who could have repaired the mortal damage done by Adam. Both Adam and Christ had a global effect upon their progeny. Adam's work resulted in sin and death; Christ's work resulted in righteousness and life. This teaching lies at the heart of any expression of Christian orthodoxy. No Christian body can claim to be orthodox or catholic which denies that Jesus Christ is the only Savior of the human race.

We should not take for granted the uniqueness of Christ as our only Savior. Some Christians live in a very limited world and they assume that other professing Christians believe essentially the same things they do. This came home to me one evening when I was speaking on the spirituality of St. Augustine in a Presbyterian church in my former hometown. I was a Presbyterian minister for eighteen years in one Presbyterian communion that held to traditional Reformed beliefs. This particular evening I was talking in another denomination of Presbyterians that differed in some significant ways from my own communion. I mentioned in passing that St. Augustine refers to Jesus as the way, the truth and the life (cf. Jn 14:6).

Afterwards, a gentlemen came up to me and complained that such a statement sounded like these fundamentalists who say that we can only find salvation through Christ. He was sure that such a great Church Father as St. Augustine could not have held such a narrow viewpoint. I assured him that St. Augustine was not a modern fundamentalist. But I also assured him that believing in Christ as the only Savior was biblical and historic Christianity and that such a great Church Father did indeed believe that Christ is the only Savior of the world. I knew that this Presbyterian denomination in which I was speaking did not formally deny Christ's unique redemption, but I also knew that this man's viewpoint represented a widespread opinion among his constituency. We should never assume that our fellow Christians know the truth about Christ our Redeemer. It is solidly founded in biblical revelation and is the historic teaching of the Catholic Church, but there are many who don't understand the full importance and impact of that belief.

Mary and the Only Savior

Mary understood that her Son was the only Savior. She knew on the basis of the Old Testament that only God could save his people. And she also knew she wasn't God. Yet the One within her womb was God, and her hope was in her Son. She knew that Jesus alone is our Redeemer, but she also knew that Jesus is never alone. His salvation, once received by others, draws them into that saving work. The redeemed of the Lord join the Lord the Redeemer in carrying out his work of redemption. They are not the original redeemers nor even parallel, equal redeemers; they are only the instruments of redemption. They cooperate with the Redeemer and therefore can be properly called redeemers in a subordinate sense. We explore that theme in the next chapter.

CHAPTER SIX

HUMAN COOPERATION IN THE PLAN OF SALVATION

Jesus Christ is the only Savior of the human race. No mere human being could ever do what he accomplished. The debt owed to God for sin is infinite because the person offended is infinite. Only an infinite person could pay a debt owed to an infinite God. Since every human being is finite, how could one of them pay this infinite debt? Yet because it was human beings that needed saving, a human being must pay the debt. And this dilemma explains the incarnation. God had to become flesh, to become a man, so that the infinite God could be joined to a human being. Because Jesus is divine, he can pay the infinite debt. Because he is man, he can pay that debt for sinful men.

Salvation is more than Christ paying the debt. It is receiving his divine life in our souls. When we are united to Christ through faith and the sacraments, we begin to acquire his presence as the sustenance of our life. In Chapter Four, we saw that the hope of God's presence was thought of as salvation in the Old Testament. John tells us that God's presence has arrived in the person of Jesus Christ, "The Word became flesh and dwelt among us." (Jn 1:14). The divine presence was hidden in the tent of Christ's flesh. Divine presence really and actually communicated something to human nature. And in the same way, the divine and the human that were in Christ are really and actually communicated to our human natures in salvation. This is what Jesus meant when he spoke of eating the flesh and drinking the blood of the Son of Man.

Salvation is more too than just receiving something. Salvation received must be passed on, and so we become God's co-workers in his plan of redemption (1 Cor 3:9). The latinate word for co-workers is *cooperators*. We cooperate in God's saving plan by extending Christ's salvation into the world. In the previous chapter, we saw how the Catholic Church teaches what the Bible clearly says, namely, that Jesus Christ is the only Savior of the world (*Solus Christus*). But the Bible also says that God's human servants can and must cooperate with his plan of salvation. In fact, without human cooperation the Gospel message cannot be spread throughout the world. This is why Jesus told his apostles that they would do greater works than he did (Jn 14:12). Jesus' earthly ministry was limited to a small corner of the world, but he gave the apostles a work to do that extended into all the world. It consisted of a sacramental ministry (baptizing) and a preaching ministry (teaching) (see Mt 28:18-20). Now the apostles were not saviors replacing Jesus' work. Their work extended his work in the world. But their work helps redeem the world by spreading his work. In this chapter, we explore the Bible's teaching on coredemption, or in other words, human cooperation in God's plan of salvation. This background is essential for understanding how the Virgin Mary held a special place in God's redemption of the world. Let's begin with some Old Testament examples.

Human Cooperation in the Old Testament: Two Examples

The Hebrew Bible is filled with examples of people who mediated between God and men, but none stands out more clearly than the "savior" of the Hebrews, Moses. Moses represented and interceded for the covenant people when they had sinned (Ex 32:30-34). Moses stood in the presence of God to receive the word he was to deliver to Israel (Ex 34). This is no doubt why the author of Hebrews compares Moses and Jesus as mediators of their respective covenants (*mesites*).

Sometimes cooperating in God's plan of salvation involves suffering. Let's consider the prophet Hosea. Hosea was called to do what no other prophet in the history was asked. The Lord told Hosea to take a prostitute as his wife (Ho 1:2) to symbolize and embody the adultery that Israel had committed against God. Israel had performed the "vilest prostitution against the Lord" (Ho 1:2) and yet they were unaware of their grievous sins. The Hebrew word used in this verse (*zanah*) is more than committing an act of adultery. It refers to a life of prostitution, of constantly giving oneself up to sexual gratification for money. It probably refers to Israel's idolatry that involved both physical and spiritual prostitution. Much pagan worship in the Ancient Near East had temple prostitutes. As Israel adopted the worship of its neighbors, it became totally attached to a way of life that had embraced the pagan practices of its neighbors and consequently forsook completely the life God was asking Israel to lead.

The message that Hosea was called to give showed how deeply the Lord had been hurt by the wife (Israel) he loved. Hosea was called to feel that pain within his own heart. Chapter 1 tells us how Hosea chose Gomer as his wife and how she bore him three children. The Lord was so intent on using Hosea to convey this message that he told him to name his three children: *Jezreel*, *Lo-Ruhamah*, and *Lo-Ammi*. As the text explains, Jezreel refers to the valley of Jezreel where Jehu slaughtered people and where God will bring an end to the house of Israel (northern kingdom). *Lo-Ruhamah* means "no compassion" and *Lo-Ammi* means "not my people."

Hosea's life was shaped completely by his relationships with his wife and children. It doesn't take much imagination to realize how Hosea must have felt. He suffered the embarrassment of everyone knowing he was a prophet of Yahweh who had a prostitute as a wife. Can you imagine the indignities that must have been cast on him? From the ungodly he must have received ridicule of the sort, "So, you're a prophet, are you?" "If you're so holy, how come you married a whore?" And from the godly he might have heard, "Hosea, we accept your message but your life doesn't measure up. You don't walk the talk. You married a disreputable woman." So Hosea had to live in the silence of knowing that the Lord had called him to a life that no one understood. Many of the great Christians of the past whom God has greatly used have had to do the same.

Consider Hosea's pain in naming his children. For those who are parents, the births of our children are days of incredible joy. Parenthood sometimes involves pain later in life, but usually the birth of a child is unmitigated joy. But Hosea's experience was completely different. The births of his children were marked with pain right from the start. Every time he looked at them, called them by name or thought of the meaning of each name, it must have brought sorrow to him. His heart must have been filled with love and deep hurt at the same time. Hosea was called to do what so many of God's servants are called to do. God often wants his servants not only to speak his message with words but with their lives. They must carry in their bodies the message they bear with their lips.

Jeremiah was called to suffer for his people Judah. This seven century prophet bore the pain of loneliness because of God's message he bore, "I sat alone because of your hand" (Jer 15:17). He was denied the normal joy of marriage and children as a sign of Judah's imminent destruction (see Jer 16:1ff). His prophetic message brought him into conflict with civil authorities and his life was threatened repeatedly:

> I was like a little lamb led to sacrifice, and I didn't know that they devised schemes against me. "Let's destroy the tree with its fruit. Let's cut him off from the land of the living, and his name won't be remembered any longer." (Jer 11:19)

> When Jeremiah finished speaking all the Lord had commanded him, the priests, the prophets, and all the people seized him with these words, "You will die." (Jer 26:8)

Jeremiah's physical suffering came to a climax when he was tossed into a dungeon by the wicked king Zedekiah. Jeremiah's sinking into the mire seems to have both a physical and spiritual connotation (Jer 38:5,6). In any case, this prophet was called to embody the message he proclaimed just as Hosea was.

Jeremiah's pain was also deeply interior. Long before the people of Judah could see the judgment of the Babylonians coming,

Jeremiah experienced the heartfelt sorrow of knowing that his beloved people and city would be destroyed:

> O my soul, my soul. I am pained in my heart. My heart makes a noise in me because of ... the alarm of war. Destruction on destruction is cried ... how long will I see the standard and hear the sound of the trumpet? (Jer 4:19)

It is hard to imagine how deep in the heart was Jeremiah's pain. But why was this painful for him? He accepted God's call to speak the divine message to a wayward people. God's word burned like fire in his bones; he had to speak. Yet he also loved his people Judah. They were God's people and he shared God's heart for his people. The conflict between knowing God's righteous standard and seeing the people's rebellion grieved him beyond words. Jeremiah's cooperation in God's plan of judgment and salvation became the single most difficult aspect of his life. But it was only a foreshadowing of the same heartache that our Savior would experience because of the obstinence of those in his day (see Mt 23:37-39).

Human Cooperation in our Lord's Teaching

Our Lord's words in the Gospels also teach us the necessity of human cooperation in salvation but to understand them we must place ourselves back into the minds of the earliest Christians. In all three Synoptic Gospels we find Jesus calling his disciples to bear the cross in his name. Consider these verses in the Gospel of Mark:

> And Jesus called the crowd along with his disciples and said to them, "If anyone wants to follow after me, let him deny himself and take up his cross and follow me. Whoever wishes to save his life will lose it. Whoever loses his life for my sake and the gospel's, he will save it. For what does it profit a man to gain the whole world and lose his soul? For what would a person give in exchange for his soul? Whoever is ashamed of me and my words in the adulterous and sinful generation, the Son of Man will be ashamed of him whenever he comes in his Father's glory with the angels." Mk 8:34-38

Imagine that you are a first century Christian living in Rome when these words were first read in church. Early church writings tell us that Mark was Peter's assistant in Rome and that his Gospel was written down from information supplied by Peter. If you were an early Christian, you would have heard about the cross many times and known that Jesus' death redeemed you from your personal sins. You would also have believed that Christ's crucifixion paid for the sins of the world.

Now when you hear Jesus' words read in church, you understand their meaning clearly. Jesus is calling you to follow in his footsteps by taking up your cross. This bearing of a cross is not optional; he says that if you don't deny yourself you will lose your life for eternity. Failure to take up the cross is the same as denying Jesus. And the one who denies Jesus will forfeit his eternal soul. But what does it mean to take up your cross? Notice that Jesus doesn't say you have to take up his cross. He says, "If anyone wants to follow me... let him take up *his own cross.*" (Mk 8:34). Why does he say this? No doubt Jesus chose the word cross to emphasize that what you do is like what he does. You are a crossbearer like he is. But it is not just any cross because the cross you bear must be one that identifies you with him. It's your identification with Jesus that may bring you shame in the world. So, if your cross is united to his cross, why does Jesus say that you must take up your own cross? He does so because he is emphasizing the need for personalizing his cross in your life. He is calling for complete identity with him even in his suffering. You must do exactly what he did. He suffered, so you must suffer.

The first three Gospels all mention Simon the Cyrenian who was compelled to help Jesus carry his cross on the way to Calvary (Mt 27:32; Mk 15:21; Lk 23:26). This is another historical detail in the Bible that goes way beyond a simple historical fact. Given the message of cross-bearing taught by Jesus earlier in each Gospel, I have little doubt that the sacred writers want us to see Simon as an example of how we should take our cross and follow Jesus. Luke's language is especially significant, "they placed the cross on him [Simon] so that he would carry it behind Jesus." (Lk 23:26). Simon is following Jesus by taking up the Master's cross. In short, following Jesus means picking up his cross and walking behind him in obedience. Simon actually helped Jesus accomplish his redemption by helping him carry the weight of the cross to Calvary. He cooperated with Jesus. So too, if we take up our cross, we will be cooperating in Jesus' redemptive work. We cannot take Christ's place, just as Simon could not, but we can help the Savior continue to bear the cross. Simon helped Jesus bear the cross *before* the fulfillment of objective redemption; we bear the cross *after* redemption has been accomplished. Our cross-bearing applies Jesus' redemption to human souls. Our imitation of his cross-bearing becomes a channel through which Jesus applies his cross and its saving power to the world.

Human Cooperation in Paul's Teaching

The apostle Paul presents us with one of the best explanations and examples of cooperation in salvation (coredemption). Paul saw himself as God's instrument of salvation for others as he explains in many places in his letters. Paul's importance cannot be overestimated. Just over half of the New Testament was written by this apostle to the Gentiles (14 of 27 books). It was Paul who took the Gospel into Europe from Palestine and he who founded the vibrant churches of Asia Minor. So important was Paul that the writer of Acts (Luke) devoted the last half of his history of the church to Paul's ministry.

Paul has several different aspects of his teaching relevant to the subject of human cooperation. Paul's teaching on the new creation (*kaine ktisis*) provides a genuine foundation for human cooperation in God's saving plan. This phrase, *new creation*, is almost like a capsule into which Paul pours an entire understanding of salvation. In both Galatians 6:15 and 2 Corinthians 5:17 Paul teaches that everyone who is in Christ is a new creation.

> Neither circumcision nor uncircumcision really means anything. Rather the new creation is what's important. (Gal 6:15)

> So, if anyone is in Christ, a new creation has occurred. Old things are gone. New things have arrived! (2 Co 5:17)

Paul uses this concept to argue that the distinctions between Jew and Gentile, as well as many others, are passé because the new entity important for the church is the new creation. We saw in the last chapter how Paul taught that union with Christ is our salvation. The new creation is yet another of Paul's ways of saying that the salvation Jesus purchased for us on the cross comes to each to us individually. It transforms Adam's race into Christ's people. But no one can be saved for us. It happens in the recesses of each human heart. Paul connects the new creation with the cross on this personal level in Galatians 6:14, the verse that immediately precedes the one quoted above, "May it never be that I would boast in anything except in the cross of our Lord Jesus Christ, through which the world was crucified to me and I to the world." So, the new creation comes about from crucifixion. Paul's language is important for he really speaks of a double crucifixion, "the world to me and I to the world." His thought goes beyond being identified with Christ. He sees himself as hanging on the cross with Christ while the world is nailed up on the cross. Paul is sandwiched between Christ and the world. He mediates Christ to the world. But then he turns the metaphor on its head and says that he is crucified to the world. Now the world is the cross and he is nailed to it. He suffers by means of the world. And his sufferings bring both him and the world closer to Christ. What was true for Paul is true for us as well. We can be God's instruments of salvation if our sinful selves are nailed to the cross. Our crosses are in the daily things of this world, but it's precisely by taking daily pains and sorrows as our crosses that we bring salvation to others.

2 Corinthians 5:17 helps us understand how being a new creation in Christ, having inner conversion, leads to salvation for others. Paul proceeds with v. 18, "All things come from God who reconciled us to himself through Christ and committed to us the ministry of reconciliation." Reconciliation unites God and us after being separated by sin. In Christ, we are reunited with God and this reunion draws us into being instruments of that grace to others. If we are new creations in Christ, we cannot help being instruments of grace for others. Paul explains with two steps. God reconciles us through Christ and Christ reconciles the world through us (2 Cor 5:19). Such language recalls Jesus' words in John 20:21-

23, "as the Father has sent me, so I send you." The mission of the apostles was from the Father mediated by Jesus. We are not the same as the apostles but we can be channels of blessing and grace for others. We can only do this task if we ourselves are recipients of grace and reconciliation.

Mary's Cooperation and Ours

Our salvation originates in only one source — *God*. Our salvation is sustained by that same source. And it will be brought to completion by the same fountain of love. Jesus Christ is the source of every blessing. But Jesus Christ calls us to cooperate with his grace in accepting, working with and perservering in his salvation. We are the recipients of his grace, but its perfection in our lives demands the assent of our wills. Yet this chapter showed something even more astounding. Not only do we cooperate with God's grace in our own salvation; we can cooperate with his grace in bringing salvation to others. This truth runs from Genesis to Revelation. Whether it was Abraham's obedience, Moses' intercession, Hosea's family pains or Paul's reconciling ministry, all these were united with and flow from the obedience of the Son of God (see Heb 5:8). If we compare Scripture with Scripture, we come away with the unmistakable fact that Mary was a woman who cooperated with God's grace to the fullest degree possible. Like any other human being, she didn't always understand God's work in her life, but she was always ready to submit her life and heart to God and his will. Let's explore that in the next chapter.

CHAPTER SEVEN

MARY IN THE PLAN OF SALVATION

The picture of Mary that arises from the pages of Scripture shows a woman whose life was totally dedicated to Jesus. In that respect, she is a model for every Christian. Mary may have been a woman with a beautiful physical appearance, but we don't really know that. One thing we can say. Mary had a beautiful soul. As we look into her soul, we find a woman who loved as few have, one who gave herself completely to the service of another, who lived a hidden and obscure life so that the light might fall upon the Light of the World, her Son. Why did God want to show us this woman? Why did he choose her to bear his Son? Is Mary's role in our lives that of an example only or is there more?

The previous three chapters (4,5,6) gave us the foundation for what we will consider here. Sometimes the Scriptures give a deep and powerful theology wrapped up in a pithy statement. Such is Paul's declaration, "when the fullness of time had come, God sent forth his Son, coming from woman, coming under the law, that he might redeem those under the law, that we might receive the adoption." (Gal 4:4). The context speaks of our being babes who did not know maturity under the Old Testament dispensation. The Mosaic law was like a tutor who led us to Christ (3:24). So, the coming of the fullness of time contrasts with the Old Testament times of preparation. But when Christ came into the world, he came and willingly submitted himself to the demands of the law because it was only by doing so that he could rescue those condemned under the law.

Why does Paul mention here that Christ was born of a woman? Paul is moving back and forth between two forms of speech: one legal, the other familial. Christ's submission to the law won those under the law. His birth from a woman adopted sinners into the same family. Jesus Christ was "born of woman ... that we might receive the adoption." Paul is probably thinking of woman generically here and so he connects Mary with the mother of all the living, Eve. There is an important parallel. Those born of Eve's race are sinners who have been expelled from the family of God. Christ's birth from a woman, who is the second Eve, brings sinners back into the family of God. This text gives us a clue as to why the Church Fathers so often spoke of Mary as the New Eve.

Salvation in the Bible is becoming a part of God's family and every family has a mother. If the church is a family, then the church must have a mother. Paul is teaching us in Galatians 4:4 that Mary is that mother. She bore Christ that we might be adopted into the same family. Since we are Jesus' brothers and sisters, we have the same mother as he did. Mary's spiritual maternity of believers is *the* foundation for everything that the Catholic Church teaches about her, but the idea that Mary is our mother is rather strange to non-Catholic Christians. Yet it is also absolutely essential for Christian unity. I return to this theme in the last chapter, but, first, we must look at Mary's privileges and calling. Then we will be in a position to understand Mary's motherhood in our lives.

Mary: Chosen and Prepared

When we consider all the Old Testament preparation for the coming of Christ, it should be not surprising that Paul says our salvation was planned by God from eternity, "even as he [God] chose us in him [Christ] before the foundation of the world, that we should be holy and blameless before him in love. He destined us to be his sons through Jesus Christ, according to the purpose of his will, to the praise of his glorious grace which he freely bestowed on us in the Beloved." (Eph 1:4,5). Since the heavenly Father is omniscient and omnipotent, it follows that his plan of salvation for the human race couldn't have been a secondary thought. But Paul speaks in even more specific terms, "He chose us in Christ his Son before he created the world." Each individual was contemplated in God's plan as the Father designed redemption. Yet if we were chosen in Christ, then Christ was also chosen by the Father. And if Christ was chosen, then the mother who bore him was also chosen.

God's choice of Mary was not an accident nor an afterthought. On the surface, it may seem that God chose Mary as one among many Jewish women he could have chosen. But when we look at Luke 1:28 carefully, we find this is not the case.

> When [Gabriel] went to her, he said, "Hail, *Full-of-Grace-One*. The Lord is with you. (Lk 1:28)

The angel Gabriel calls Mary by a new and unprecedented title, *Full-of-Grace-One*. This word is sometimes translated "highly favored" but such a translation is probably more a reading of theology into the text than drawing the meaning out of it. Rarely have most Christians understood this word. The original Greek word *kecharitomene* is a perfect passive participle used substantively. This substantive (noun) use means that it is used as a title such as when we call someone "the winner" or "the victor." It represents a title of someone because of what that person has achieved. Only in Mary's case, the achievement is not something she did, but something that was done to her. She was passive. She was fully graced.

Kecharitomene is also used in the perfect tense which means that Mary was already in a fully graced state when the angel Gabriel came to speak to her. Sometime in the past, she was made complete in grace and she was still in that condition when Gabriel spoke. So, God chose Mary to be the mother of his Son because he had already prepared (predestined) her for this role by making her complete in grace.

The particular way in which verse twenty-eight is arranged also indicates that *kecharitomene* is meant to be a title. Normally in the ancient world, someone great would be addressed with the word "Hail" followed by a title. "Hail Caesar" was a common form of address to the Roman emperor because Caesar was a title, not a personal name. This is why Jesus is mocked with the words, "Hail, King of the Jews" (Mt 27:29). When God's messenger Gabriel addresses Mary as *Full-of-Grace-One*, he is giving her a title, one that had never been used of any other woman. "Hail, *Perfected-In-Grace-One*" becomes her unique title just as "King of the Jews" becomes Jesus' title. And this shows God's choice of Mary was no accident.

God did not look down one day and say, "I need a woman through whom to give my Son to the world." His choice of Mary was made long before Mary was ever born. In fact, since God's decrees are eternal, then his decree to redeem the world in Christ is eternal. His choice of his Son is eternal. But then his choice of his Son's mother is also eternal. Because God knew in the secret places of eternity the woman who would bear the Son of God, he also prepared that woman ahead of time by making her *full-of-grace* or *perfected-in-grace*.

The writer of Hebrews confirms this when he quotes Psalm 40:6 from the Greek version of the Old Testament, "Sacrifice and offering You did not desire but a body you have prepared for me." (Heb 10:5). The body Jesus assumed in his becoming a man was prepared by God the Father so that God the Son could make a perfect offering of his body on the cross. It was Jesus' offering of his body that makes us holy, "We have been made holy through the sacrifice of the *body* of Jesus Christ once for all." (Hb 10:10). Yet Jesus' body was not a blind concoction of cells, bones and skin. Everything that Jesus' body was came from Mary. Just as the perfect sacrifice of Jesus was no accident, the preparation of that body for the sacrifice was no accident. And just as the preparation of Jesus' body was planned by God, the preparation of the woman who would give him that body was planned by God too.

God chose Mary to be the mother of his Son *before* he created the world just as he chose us in Christ before the foundation of the world (cf. Eph 1:4). And this woman he chose, he also prepared by making her *perfect or complete in grace* before Gabriel spoke to her on that joyful day of the annunciation of Christ's being conceived in her womb. When Gabriel spoke to her, he called her by a title that fit her perfectly, a woman complete in grace. This is the meaning of the words *immaculate conception* that have been used from very early times in the Christian Church. Mary's heart and womb were prepared by the grace of God to bear the Son of God. The benefits of Jesus' death on the cross were completely applied to her from the very moment of conception in the womb of her mother. It was that perfectly graced heart which said YES to God ("be it done to me according to your word" Lk 1:38).

Mary was conceived in the womb of her mother without the stain of original sin because Christ her Son perfectly redeemed her. All of us are redeemed by the same work of Christ, but his saving work is applied to us progressively throughout our life. In Mary's case, Christ applied his saving work retroactively, as it were, and preserved her from the stain of sin. Christ is her Savior as much as he is ours, but that salvation was applied in a different manner in her case. Why was this necessary? Why was it important for Mary to be immaculately conceived? *Because of the One who would dwell within her body.* All that we have learned in the previous chapters about the plan of salvation points to this truth — the temple of God must be holy and prepared for the coming of God's presence. Salvation is more than God forgiving us. It is even more than Christ's death on the cross, though that is the singular event of history. Salvation is God's dwelling in the midst of his people forever. It is the union of God's people to God. God the Son united his divine nature to our humanity. John puts it poignantly, "the Logos became flesh and tabernacled among us." (Jn 1:14). And the tabernacle of the Most High wherein the Son of God lived was the flesh he took from the womb of the Virgin Mary. His holiness demanded a fit dwelling place, one that was pure enough for his holiness.

Obedience Training: Following her Son's Steps

Mary didn't understand all the ramifications of her YES to God. She still had much to learn. And here we find a striking parallel with Jesus. The writer of Hebrews tells us that Jesus "learned obedience from the things he suffered." (Heb 5:8). Consider how remarkable this truth is. Why did the perfect Son of God have to learn to obey? Why did the spotless Lamb of God require suffering to gain obedience? Jesus "offered up both prayers and requests to him who could save him from death." (Heb 5:7). Surely the author must be thinking of Gethsemane where our Lord gave forth "great cries and tears." The biblical writer no doubt wants to stress the complete humanity of God the Son. His life was no phantasm. He lived a truly human existence. And what did he gain from this trodding of the human path? "He learned obedience from his sufferings and once perfected became the source of eternal salvation to all who obey him" (Heb 5:8,9). His sinless person (cf. Heb 4:15) and his status as Son ("although he was a son") did not prevent him from having to suffer and be humiliated for the salvation of others. His perfectly human life was not just one without sin. It was a life of active suffering. And by those sufferings he granted salvation to those who look to him.

If Mary was immaculately conceived, why did she have to learn obedience? For the same reason her divine Son did. She joined him in his sufferings and humiliation so that he (the source) might make her the channel of grace in the lives of his followers. Recall Simeon's words to Mary again, "and a sword will pierce your very own soul that the thoughts of many hearts may be revealed." (Luke 2:35). I will return to this text in more detail in the last chapter, but it is clear that Simeon connects Mary's sufferings intimately with those of Jesus (see Lk 2:34). And the result is that many are confronted with a decision about Jesus' salvation. We saw the principle of human cooperation in Chapter Six. Here we see it in its highest form. Mary cooperated with her Son's saving mission by entering into his sufferings, the same ones that made him the source of eternal salvation to all who follow him. If he, the divine Son of God, needed to learn obedience to be perfected, how much more his mother, a human creature, needed to walk the path of obedience to find her final glory. And she found that glory as a gift bestowed by the resurrection of Christ her Son.

Mary Shares Christ's Glory: The Assumption

Mary's role in the plan of salvation on earth leads naturally to the climax of heaven. What we have seen so far suggests that Mary's unique part in the saving work of Jesus her Son is made richer and fuller by a continuing ministry in heaven. How could she, whom

God called most blessed among women, finish her ministry by a simple earthly death when she was bound intimately to her Son from eternity? Could earthly power separate what God had joined together? What Simeon foretold — that Mary would share in the sufferings of her Son (Lk 2:35) — implied that Jesus' mother would also share in his glory. Present suffering and future glory are always tightly linked in the New Testament. When Paul told of his own wishes, he saw the unbreakable chain of "knowing the power of His [Christ's] resurrection and the fellowship of His sufferings" (Phil 3:10). In the same vein, Paul knew that "the sufferings of the present age were not worthy of being compared to the glory to be revealed to us." (Rom 8:18). Present suffering leads to eternal glory. It is this fundamental truth that underlies Mary's being assumed body and soul into heaven.

It is sometimes thought, even by Catholic theologians, that there is no clear evidence in the Bible for Mary's bodily assumption into heaven. But this thinking results from looking for the wrong kind of evidence. At this point, fundamentalism and historical-critical scholarship make strange bedfellows because both are looking for explicit statements of Mary's assumption while missing the force of the message of redemption. Earthly redemption leads to heavenly glory throughout the New Testament. The cross gains the crown (cf. 2 Tim 4:7,8). If Mary shared her Son's sufferings, she surely shared his glory.

The assumption of Mary into heaven is based on the clear teaching of Scripture applied to that woman who was blessed above all women. This principal — that *the redeemed of the Lord share the glory of the Lord* — takes on several different nuances in the Bible, but all teach that what is the Lord's becomes ours through faith. In fact, the essence of salvation contains the truth that Jesus' suffering and glory becomes ours eventually. This is why Paul says in Romans 8:17 that we are "joint heirs with Christ, if indeed we suffer with Him that we also might be glorified with Him."

Sharing Christ's glory is a reward for identifying with Him on earth. Paul uses the military and athletic metaphors in his pastoral letters to Timothy and Titus, showing unmistakably the notion of reward:

> My life is already spent and the time of my departure
> has arrived. I have fought the good fight. I have finished
> the race. I have kept the faith. Finally, a crown of righ-
> teousness awaits me with which the Lord will reward
> (*apodosei*) me on that day. (2 Tim 4: 6-8a)

Fighting the good fight, waging warfare, was Paul's example to
Timothy, whom he encouraged to contend for the faith (see 1 Tim
1:18; 6:12). When Paul exhorted Timothy to "suffer hardship as a
good soldier of Christ Jesus" (2 Tim 2:3), he did so on the basis of
God's principle of reward for suffering. Our Lord Jesus also spoke
of heavenly glory as a reward for service on earth in the parable of
sheep and goats (Mt 25:31-46). The basis on which the sheep inherit the kingdom prepared from the foundation of the world *is*
the loving service they rendered to misfortunates in this life because Christ was, as it were, hiding in the poor and disadvantaged
(see 35,36). Likewise, it is he who "does the will of my Father in
heaven" (Mt 7:21) who receives Christ's welcoming words. The
correlation between work and reward, between service and glory,
is unmistakable.

What does it mean to share Christ's glory? For example, the
privilege of sharing in Christ's judgment is given to those who follow Jesus. The Lord Jesus promised the apostles, "whenever the
Son of Man sits upon his throne, then you also will sit twelve thrones
judging the twelve tribes of Israel." (Mt 19:28). Paul goes further
in asking, "don't you know that the saints will judge the angels?"
(I Co 6:2). Sharing Christ's glory also means being united with
God. Recall that Jesus prayed for his disciples to share in the same
glory that he has with the Father (Jn 17:24). Our final union with
Christ in his glory begins by being united with his suffering on
earth. All Christian suffering, if offered to the Father in heaven, is
redemptive because our suffering is united to that of Jesus. And
this pattern of present suffering and future glory is what explains
the teaching of the Catholic Church on Mary's assumption.

Mary was redeemed the same way all of us are, by the death
and resurrection of Christ. Paul assures us that Christ's resurrection secures our bodily resurrection to eternal life (I Co 15:20-23).
But the resurrected life is not simply a future benefit. The power of

that risen life is ours *now* through baptism and faith (see Rom 6:4,5). Our power to overcome sinful habits of our old nature comes from the resurrection life of Christ (Rom 6:11). So, Mary the Christian also had that resurrection life within her. As we have seen, she had it to the fullest degree possible from the moment of her conception in her mother's womb. If Mary died a *normal* earthly death, her body would have to await the general resurrection like any other Christian. But the assumption of Mary means that she shared her Son's resurrection life before her death, or at least before her body decayed. The power and reality of Mary's bodily assumption into heaven came from Jesus' resurrection. Why was this fitting? To show us on earth what our future destiny will be. Mary's assumption is *a constant sign of our future resurrection.* And it was completely fitting for Jesus to do this for his mother. She not only gave him birth; she shared his sufferings to an unimaginable degree. And if she suffered with him, it was fitting for her to share his glory in anticipation of us. (cf. Rom 8:17)

Mary: Mediatrix of Every Blessing

It is very difficult for many Christians to understand, much less embrace, the idea that Mary is the mediatrix of every blessing from God (sometimes called mediatrix of all graces). Christians of all stripes find this title questionable because it seems to usurp the unique position of Jesus Christ as the only mediator between God and man. Aren't we belittling the saving work of Jesus by saying that Mary is also a mediatrix (feminine for mediator) of every blessing that God wants to give his human family? Doesn't 1 Timothy 2:5 say that Christ Jesus is the one mediator between God and us? And doesn't the book of Hebrews tell us that Jesus Christ is the one who intercedes for us at the right hand of God while it says nothing about Mary?

A word of caution is in order. The immaculate conception and the assumption of Mary are on the highest level of authority. The Catholic Church has defined the immaculate conception and the assumption to be dogmas of faith which no faithful Catholic can disbelieve or disregard. Mary as the mediatrix of all graces does not enjoy that defined, infallible status. But it is a doctrine which has been taught for centuries within the Church. The same may be said of Mary as coredemptrix. Mary as mediatrix and coredemptrix have not been declared infallible dogmas. Notice that doesn't mean they are not infallible, but only that the Church has not yet been convinced of their infallible status. If and when the official teachers of the Church (i.e. the bishops) — and especially the highest teacher, the Universal Pastor — become convinced that these titles of Mary are part of divine revelation, then the Church will define these doctrines as infallible truths to be believed by every Catholic. But such a declaration will be based on long and thorough study of Holy Scripture, the history of dogma and devotion and the universal worship of the Church (liturgy).

Even though I know the difficulties that many non-Catholic Christians have with calling Mary mediatrix and coredemptrix, I have become convinced that these are concepts well grounded in Scripture and the history of Christian thought. All the legitimate questions that may be raised don't in any way minimize Mary's role as mediatrix because it is a completely biblical concept. Mary's mediating position flows from God's grace and gifts that come to us only through her Son Jesus Christ. Since Jesus is the fullness of God's grace, Mary is a mediatrix because she brings Jesus' fullness to us. Consider Paul's statements about Jesus' fullness in the book of Colossians. Col 2:9 says, "All the fullness of the deity dwells in him bodily." (see also 1:19). "Jesus Christ is the image of the invisible God, the first born of all creation." (Col 1:15). The thought of Christ being the source of every blessing is what moves Paul to say that "you were washed, you were sanctified, you were justified in the name of our Lord Jesus Christ and in the Spirit of our God." In short, whatever blessing God wants to give us comes through his Son Jesus Christ because every promise of God is yes and amen in Christ (see 2 Co 1:20).

If the fullness of grace and salvation comes through Jesus Christ, then it follows that Jesus' fullness comes through Mary because the only way Jesus has come to our world is through her. John tells that in Jesus becoming a man, "grace and truth came through him" (Jn 1:17). Jesus had the fullness of God's blessing from the very moment of his conception. If the fullness of divine grace was there in that moment when the Holy Spirit created the perfect God-man in Mary's womb (Lk 1:35,36), then that divine grace was mediated by Mary's womb and heart. The love she had for her divine Son could be no less than what every mother feels for the child created within her. Yet *her* gift to her Son far exceeded her biological heritage; she gave herself completely to and for Jesus when she said to Gabriel, "let it be to me as you have said" (Lk 1:38). She united her soul and body to the fullness of God's grace that was living and growing within her body. Whenever anyone accepts Jesus in all his fullness, he receives unimaginable blessing and becomes a channel or mediator of blessing to others. No one in human history has been so completely united with Jesus in his fullness as Mary his mother. The wealth of blessings that God placed in Jesus Christ was received by Mary. She thereby became a mediatrix of that God-man who had every blessing in himself.

Another scriptural theme reinforces the reality of Mary as mediatrix — Mary as the New Eve. We saw in Chapter Five how Paul developed the parallelism between Adam and Christ. Though Paul never uses the phrase *Christ as the New Adam*, his teaching justifies it. Christ's obedience untied the knot of Adam's disobedience. The sin and death Adam brought into the world was overcome and destroyed by Christ (1 Co. 15:22). But recall too that Romans 5:15-17 emphasized that Jesus' saving work far exceeded Adam's transgression. Adam's act of disobedience brought all into judgment but Christ's act of obedience brought an abundance of life by his own death.

What are the implications of this Adam-Christ parallelism? One implication that many modern Christians never consider is about Mary. I too was completely ignorant of this implication for the first thirty-eight years of my life even though I had read and taught much theology. The Fathers of the Church in the early centuries of Christianity knew this truth well. They often spoke of Mary as the New Eve because she was intimately tied to the saving work of Jesus as the New Adam. It became proverbial in the early Church to say that the knot of Eve's disobedience was untied by Mary's obedience to the Lord (see Lk 1:38).

Is there any biblical justification for this extension of the Adam-Christ parallelism into the Eve-Mary connection? First, let's consider Genesis 3:15 where God speaks to the serpent after Adam and Eve have fallen into sin:

> And I will put enmity between you [serpent] and the woman
> and between your offspring and hers;
> he will crush your head
> and you strike his heel.

From earliest Christian times, this verse has been understood as the first announcement of the gospel of salvation (*protoevangelium*). The narrative of the fall into sin in Genesis Chapter Three makes it clear that Eve participated in the first sin of humanity with a full consent of her will. Adam, not Eve, was the covenant head of humanity but she cooperated in Adam's disobedience by her own disobedience to the word of God (Gen 3:6). Eve was not the innocent victim of circumstances nor was she simply an ignorant instrument of Satan's deception. As Adam's willful disobedience enslaved humanity (Rom 5:12-14), so Eve's willful cooperation in his sin made her a guilty accomplice in the sin that ruined our relationship with God. If Eve had been just an insignificant bystander, God would never have pronounced the curses on her that Scripture records (Genesis 3). Paul says explicitly that "sin entered the world through one man and death came through sin." (Rom 5:12). Genesis Chapter Three tells us that Eve cooperated with Adam in those deadly consequences. She along with Adam was a mediatrix of sin and death. Adam, we might say, was *the Sinner*. Eve was *the Co-Sinner*.

Genesis 3:15 speaks of the enmity between the woman and the serpent. It predicts a war to the death between the serpent's (Satan) offspring and the offspring of the woman. No searching reader of the Bible can doubt that the seed of the woman that will crush Satan's head is Christ. If Christ is the seed of the woman, then the woman is none other than Mary. So, the verse predicts a mortal conflict between Satan and his seed on the one side and Mary and her seed on the other. The woman in Genesis 3:15 does not have to be Mary alone. In fact, it may refer to both Eve and Mary. Eve is the first mother of the living (Gen 3:20); Mary is the mother of the One who gives life to all (cf. Jn 14:6). What was true of Eve is even more true of Mary just as what was true of Adam was even more true of Christ. Eve's disobedience brought sin and death; Mary's obedience brought righteousness and life. Jesus was Mary's Son and he is the bringer of righteousness and life. Jesus, we might say, is the *Redeemer*; Mary is the *Co-Redeemer*.

The idea that we could call Mary a coredemptrix with Jesus her Son should not be strange at all if you have followed the discussion of the preceding chapters. By the term coredemptrix we mean that Mary cooperated with her Son's saving purpose. We have seen that idea all through the Scriptures. Paul saw himself as a coredeemer by his involvement in the reconciling ministry of the Church (2 Cor 5:18-21). Paul never saw himself as usurping what Christ has done. Paul's redeeming ministry was only possible because of Christ's redemption. Paul's work simply extended what Jesus had already done. Paul even saw his own suffering as contributing to Christ's redeeming his body, the Church (see Col 1:24). Jesus communicated the grace of his suffering to Paul so Paul could join in his reconciling and redeeming work. If this was true of Paul, how much more is it true of Mary. Paul was one among many apostles, but Mary was unique in bearing the Son of God. And only Mary fulfills the role that corresponds to Eve. If Christ is the New Adam as Paul teaches, then Mary is the New Eve as the Church Fathers teach.

Mary's role as the New Eve is why the Catholics use the term mediatrix for Jesus' mother. It may seem strange and unbiblical to say that we come to Jesus through Mary but consider again the divine plan of salvation. With his infinite power, God the Father could have given us his Son the same way he gave the first man Adam, by a fiat creation that did not involve human conception and birth. God could have created a body for his Son out of nothing. But in his infinite wisdom, God the Father chose one of his daughters, Mary, to give the gift of herself to his Son. Whatever constitutes the physical, human nature of the Son of God, he received it from Mary. So, to say we go to Jesus through Mary is simply to walk the path in reverse that God the Father laid down for us. *We come to Jesus the same way he came to us — through Mary.* In her arms she held the entire fountain of all mercy, grace and love when she held him that night of his birth in Bethlehem. By her voluntary presence at the cross, Mary offered her Son to us as the Redeemer of the world. Jesus is the source of all graces; Mary is the medium (mediatrix) through which the graces come. To believe this is only to be obedient to the plan of salvation God the Father established. To reject it is to spurn God's chosen plan of salvation.

Surely, though, it is an unwarranted conclusion to say that Mary mediates between us and Jesus when 1 Timothy 2:5 explicitly says that "there is one God and one mediator between God and man, the man Christ Jesus." Doesn't calling Mary, or any human being, a mediator, add to Christ's perfect redemptive work and thereby minimize the uniqueness of his saving grace? Doesn't Paul's language of Jesus Christ as the one mediator exclude other mediators? Surely, no Christian would want to detract from the unique role of Christ as our Redeemer and Mediator. How then can the Catholic Church countenance the title of mediatrix applied to Mary?

A closer examination of 1 Timothy 2:5 suggests quite the opposite from what this objection supposes. As always, it is crucial to interpret biblical verses in context, both immediate and far. In 1 Tim 2:1 Paul commands that prayers be made for all kinds of people. Among these prayers are intercessions. Paul especially urges intercession for those in authority so that Christians may lead quiet and holy lives (v 2). Our deepest motivation for living a quiet life of prayer is twofold: it pleases God and it may lead others to a knowledge of the truth (see vss 3,4).

It is in this context that Paul reminds us of the foundation of our hope. What confidence do we have that a sacrificial life of prayer on our part will lead others to salvation? Our confidence is in the one God whom we worship and in his Son, Jesus Christ, who is the one appointed mediator between God and man (vs 5). Why does Paul remind us that there is one mediator between God and man in this context? No doubt Paul wants us to understand that our intercession, that is, our acts of mediation, are based on the one mediatorship of the man Christ Jesus. It is interesting that Paul doesn't say that the one mediator is Christ Jesus. Rather, he says that the one mediator between God and man is *the man* Christ Jesus. The mediator between God and man had to be a man, or he couldn't be a mediator. It is Christ in his humanity who mediates between us and the Father.

Now if Christ's mediation as the perfect God-man excluded any other human mediation, why would Paul urge us to pray for others in the hope that it might bring them to salvation? Does this mean that we are saviors competing with Christ our Lord? Not at all! In fact, Paul is reminding us that any mediation on our part has no significance or power apart from Christ's eternal mediation. This is why Paul adds concerning Jesus that he "gave himself a ransom for all." (vs 6). Christ's death on Calvary was the greatest act of mediation that provides the foundation for all other human mediation.

Thus 1 Timothy 2:5, far from excluding human mediation, encourages it by showing us the foundation of all human mediation in the one, unique mediatorial work of Jesus Christ. Christ in his sacred humanity rescued us from hopelessness and the power of the evil one. We too through our prayers and holy lives may bring hope to others, not a hope that originates in us, but one and the same hope that comes from Jesus Christ. And this is what calling Mary a mediatrix means.

Another reason why 1 Timothy 2:5 doesn't exclude human mediation is because the Scriptures elsewhere call human beings mediators. Paul himself calls Moses a mediator of the old covenant in Gal 3:19. Paul says that "the law ... was commanded through angels by the hand of a mediator." The law of which Paul speaks is the old covenant that came through the mediation of Moses. And clearly the Old Testament priests functioned as mediators between the people of Israel and God. Now it may be said that Christ, the mediator of the new covenant (Heb 12:23), has superseded these human mediators so that they are no longer necessary. *The Epistle to the Hebrews* confirms this when it says that Christ's priesthood has made the Old Testament priesthood obsolete. Theirs was the partial; his is the perfect priesthood. But Christ was still the mediator for the people of Israel as he is for us. The old covenant people of God were not saved by the sacrifices of bulls and goats (see Heb 9:12,13; 10:11); they were saved by the same Christ who died for us. So, if having human priests as mediators in the old covenant was not incompatible with Christ being the supreme mediator, neither is it incompatible for us as the new covenant people of God.

It should be remembered that the Catholic Church teaches *both* the unique, redemptive mediatorship of Jesus Christ *and* the subordinate mediatorship of his mother Mary. Mary's mediation for us as Christians means that she prays for us and pleads our cause for the throne of grace in heaven. She does what we all should want to do, namely, be an instrument of salvation by our prayers in the lives of others.

All the privileges God granted to Mary flow from her calling to be the mother of the Savior. She was chosen for this singular task so that she might share in her Son's salvation, both as recipient and as helper. Once she conceived Jesus in her womb, she was never the same. She had been already blessed with the highest degree of God's grace, but she probably began to understand the reason only on the day Gabriel came to her. Her own walk of faith was molded by her attachment to her Son and his saving mission. Even at the end of Jesus' life, Mary was devoted to his work. Her inseparable union with Jesus is what makes her a mediatrix of all graces that come from him. She shared his sufferings by cooperating in his salvation (coredemptrix). Now she shares his glory in heaven, not in soul only, but in body and soul. Her exalted position came from the lowly spirit that said what each of us must say, "let it be done to me as you have said." (Lk 1:38).

CHAPTER EIGHT

MARY, CHRISTIAN UNITY AND THE EUCHARIST

All I have said about Mary in the previous seven chapters points to the unbreakable link she has with Christ her Son. All that Mary is came from Jesus, her Lord and ours. But the question no doubt lingers: what does Mary have to do with Christian unity? Granted that Mary is indispensable for understanding Jesus, how is it necessary to speak of Mary to achieve unity among professing Christians? To place Mary and Christian unity in the same sentence is foreign to many Christians, both non-Catholic and Catholic.

Recall for a moment the underlying patterns that have emerged from our survey of Scripture. Why did God have to send his Son to be born of a virgin in order to redeem the world? Why did the Logos, the eternal Son of God, have to take a human nature? Why, in short, was there an Incarnation? The answer to that question goes to the heart of the question: what is salvation? The *Logos* had to become flesh and dwell among us (Jn 1:14-18) because he had to communicate his divine life to our human nature. Salvation is more than a legal declaration of innocence. Eternal life is not only a legal transaction exchanging Christ's righteousness for our sinfulness. Salvation is a gift of life to dead people. It is God's giving himself to us in order that we might share his trinitarian life. This has been celebrated in the historical liturgies when in one way or another it is said: *may we come to share in the divinity of Christ who humbled himself to share in our humanity.* Salvation is a communication of real grace, and grace is not only an attitude of favor toward sinners. It is a bestowal, a donation of something that is real, of an entity that is nothing less than God's own life within the human soul. This is why the eternal Logos had to become a man: so that he might communicate to human nature his divine life and love. Salvation is not just being forgiven of sin. It is being united to God himself. This union with God requires perfection (Mt 5:48) because only the pure in heart will experience the beatific vision (see Mt 5:8). As God the Father communicates his life to us more fully, we grow closer to that holiness without which no one will see the Lord (Heb 12:14). But how is this divine life, this holiness given to us?

Mary as Mother of the Church

Uniting our lives to God the Father is not done without a mother. On the natural level, we are biological offspring of our father and mother, carrying within us the genetic makeup of both our parents. And salvation is joining a family. The Bible uses the models of both natural birth and adoption to describe this process. Adoption places us in the legal realm, reminding us that God the Father has brought alien sinners into his own family and made them his own. But we are also born into the family of God through baptism (Jn 1:13,3:5). We are the *real* children of God by rebirth through the washing of the water in the word (Eph 5:26). This model of natural birth means that we increasingly take on the divine life of God the Father communicated to us by the death and resurrection of God the Son. Now every family also has a mother and this is the reason why the Church has always thought of Mary as the mother of all Christians. She gave birth to her Firstborn in her virginity, but Jesus was not her only Son. Jesus was her only physical child, but Mary has many children who she bore and who she continues to nurture with her maternal care.

Paul seems to have this idea clearly in mind when he says in Romans 8:28, 29, "we know that all things work together for good for those who love God, for those who are called in accord with his plan because those he foreknew, he also predestined to be conformed to the image of his Son that he might be the firstborn among many brethren." To conform to something is to make it the same shape as the original (Greek *summorphos*). Thus we are predestined for the purpose of looking like Jesus Christ, says Paul, of being molded into his image. The word translated *image* in this text is the Greek *eikon* from which we derive the word *icon* in English. An icon is an image that also embodies what it represents. We are to embody Jesus Christ by gradually taking on his image in our lives. Paul is clearly thinking of this molding process as a period of gestation and birth because he says that its purpose is "that He [Christ] might be the firstborn among many brethren." The purpose of the Father's predestination is to produce many sons and daughters who all look alike, or more specifically, who all look like the firstborn Son.

Consider how Jesus Christ came to look the way he did. How was his life shaped and formed? He was born after being molded and formed in Mary's womb. If God the Father wishes our lives to be formed in Christ's image, isn't it necessary to go through the same molding process He experienced? This is why St. Augustine says that the predestined are also shaped and formed in Mary's womb. Her womb is the place, the locale where we are molded into the image of Christ her firstborn Son. Christ's formation in Mary's womb was physical under the guidance of the Holy Spirit (Lk 1:35). Our formation is spiritual but under the guidance of that same Holy Spirit, *and* in the same locale, the womb of the Virgin.

The process of being conformed into Christ's image through implantation in Mary's womb takes place not only on an individual level, but on a corporate level as well. The whole body of the Church is being conformed into Christ by being placed in Mary's womb. As mother of the church, Mary cares deeply for the spiritual growth of every member. She wishes her sons and daughters to be conformed to her firstborn Son's image because she knows that Christ alone will be able to unify the church. And Mary is also the symbol of the church as our mother. The ancient Fathers so often spoke of the church as our mother because they knew that it was in the womb of the church that we find Christ. And so the church's pastors have always spoken with maternal concern for God's people. Paul himself reflects this maternal love in Galatians 4:19 "my dear children, for whom I am in birth pangs until Christ is formed in you..." The church through its pastoral ministry shapes each Christian into the image of Christ and more deeply into the body of Christ. The body of Christ is both a fact and also in the process of being formed. And that is why we must acknowledge Mary as our spiritual mother in order to have unity in its fullest expression. In her womb, as it were, the mystical body of Christ is being formed into the image of the fullness of her firstborn Son.

Unity among Christians will be empty and vain unless it is accompanied by the kind of solidarity Mary showed with the sufferings of her Son. Recall how in Chapter Two we saw Mary's presence at the crucifixion as an act of her cooperation with Jesus in his suffering. She willingly gave up her Son as the world's Redeemer and felt the depth of pain in her own heart. Simeon's words to Mary, — "a sword will also pierce your soul" (Lk 2:35) — spoken some thirty-three years earlier, finally came to their agonizing fulfillment in her life. Mary completely identified herself with her Son's saving mission, and she freely took on her role as mother of the church ("behold your son"). Her solidarity with the suffering church calls us to a radical solidarity with suffering Christians all over. When we see ourselves as united to the sufferings of the church, we will understand that they are nothing less than Christ's own sufferings. Jesus is completely identified with his hurting people (see Mt 25:31-46 esp. v.40; Acts 9:5; Col 1:24). It is a little known fact that more Christians have been martyred for their faith in the twentieth century than in all previous centuries combined. This is partly because of the greater absolute number of Christians today, but it does underscore how the sufferings of Christians now have not been mitigated by our much touted tolerance of modern democracies. If we hurt for our fellow Christians, as we should, how much more does the mother of the church weep for her children!

Scripture adds another aspect to Mary's suffering motherhood of the Church that we must not miss. Let's look at Simeon's words to Mary again:

> (v34) Behold this [child] is set for the fall and rising of many in Israel and for a sign to be contradicted. (v35) And a sword will also pierce your very own soul that the thoughts of many hearts may be revealed. (Lk 2:34,35).

These verses are actually distorted in several English translations by taking the last phrase ("that the thoughts of many hearts may be revealed") and moving it to the end of v34 so that the revealing of the thoughts of many hearts results from the sign to be contradicted rather than from the piercing of Mary's soul. *But there is no objective basis for such a transposition in the original Greek text or manuscripts.* I wonder if this is an instance where theological orientation has influenced translation.

Let us take the text as it stands and ask what it tells us about Jesus and Mary. Simeon's words without a doubt have the flavor of a prophecy. They foretell how this child will be the crucial turning point at which people must respond positively or negatively to God's salvation. Those who reject God's salvation will speak against this sign. It is that rejection of her Son that will pierce Mary's heart, not only in the normal maternal sense of a mother who wants her Son honored, but also in the sense of seeing many of God's people turn away from salvation to their own destruction. Mary wept at the cross because her Son died an ignominious death, but she also wept for her people who rejected her Son's saving mission.

How does that piercing of Mary's soul reveal the thoughts of many hearts? The word translated thoughts (*dialogismoi*) is used thirteen times in the New Testament and always with a pejorative meaning "bad,evil thoughts." This suggests that the thoughts to be revealed will be directed against the child who is the hated sign, and possibly against his mother as well. Consider carefully the progression of thought in verses 34 and 35. The child in Simeon's arms is established as the turning point in the history of salvation. Some will respond favorably, others unfavorably. For the first group, this Messiah will be the joy of God's people. For the second group, he will be their destruction. How? Not because the child wishes their destruction, but because they choose to contradict his ministry. He is the sign of salvation, the banner of God's kingdom. Everyone who opposes him will be lost. This situation will affect not only the child Messiah himself, but also his mother. The Messiah's mother is so intimately bound to his life and ministry that any pain connected to his ministry affects her in the deepest part of her soul. Now, however, we learn the purpose of this entire situation — "that the evil thoughts of many hearts will be revealed." As the Messiah of Israel sets up his kingdom and asks his mother to share in his ministry, the evil thoughts of those who oppose him and his mother are revealed.

What could such truths mean except that Mary's motherhood of Jesus our Lord is an integral part of his plan of salvation? The revelation of those who accept Jesus' salvation in humility and those who reject him comes about *through his mother's heartfelt sufferings*. Surely this means that Mary's motherhood of believers is an indispensable part of Jesus' plan of salvation. No family is without a mother, and Jesus' messianic family has no less. Only Jesus didn't choose just any woman to be that mother of the messianic family. He chose his own mother. And that is why we must receive Mary as our spiritual mother if we want to be a part of Christ's plan of salvation. By looking to Mary as the pierced soul, we see her family the church in greater clarity because the thoughts of many hearts are revealed by her sufferings flowing from those of Jesus her Son.

Now let us return to unity. Think first of all of how Jesus and Mary are united. From that moment when the Holy Spirit created in her womb the body of Jesus, their two lives could never be separated. What Mary gave to Jesus he will always have. He will never again be without his body, his human soul and his human nature. He is forever the God-Man. And his sacred humanity, including his body, is our salvation. There is only one Jesus, one Shepherd. There can be only one flock (Jn 10:16). But neither is Mary the same since that day of her conception of Jesus in her womb. What Jesus gave to Mary she will always have. He gave her fullness of grace. He gave her the fullness of the Spirit. He gave her the most important relationship she would ever have — Mother and Son. But he also gave her as a mother to his disciples, his brothers and sisters who would follow in his footsteps. And as there is only one Savior, so there is only one family of the Savior. And every family has only one mother. Mary's motherhood of believers is Jesus' gift of his closest and dearest relation to those whom he loves. Just as Jesus is the source of unity for Christians, so Mary in her role as mother of the Church is the instrument of unity for us all.

Mary and the Unity of the Trinity

The unity we seek does not result from negotiated agreements. Our Christian unity must be founded on truth. It must be unity of heart and mind, a permanent oneness that is not shaken by the changing tides of custom and culture. The New Testament concept of unity is nothing less than union with the Holy Trinity. Jesus our Lord prayed that the oneness of his disciples would be like and flow from the oneness experienced by the Father, Son and Holy Spirit: "that they all may be one, Father, as you are in me and I in you that they may also be one in us." (Jn 17:21). Jesus Christ does not want our unity to be *like* his and the Father's. He wants our unity to be *the same* as he and the Father have.

Mary is both a sign and an instrument of the unity coming from the Holy Trinity because she bears a unique relation to each member. Let's see how Mary is related to the Father, the Son and the Holy Spirit. First, however, a word of caution. In A.D. 431 the ancient Christian church defined Mary as the Mother of God because the church wanted to protect the full divinity and humanity of Jesus Christ. This title, Mother of God (or better God-bearer), asserted that the child in Mary's womb was nothing less than fully God and fully man. But the title Mother of God never was nor should be interpreted to mean that Mary is the mother of the Trinity. Mary bears a distinct relation to each member of the Trinity, but she is not the mother of the Father, nor of the Holy Spirit.

Mary is the daughter of the Father. When Mary proclaims herself the handmaiden of the Lord (Lk 1:38,48), she is declaring her filial obedience to the will of God. The love she has for the heavenly Father shows itself in her desire to be his vessel of bringing salvation to the world. What better sign of unity than this act of submission to the will of God? If we only follow Mary's lead, we will find ourselves united in heart as her heart was united with the heavenly Father's heart. She did not negotiate with God, bargain with him nor seek a compromise. She acknowledged her dependence on his grace and sought to perform his bidding. The will of the Father is unity for us who profess his Son. We will only have unity when we have submitted ourselves to the Father like Mary.

Yet Mary is more than a sign. She is an instrument of unity. How is this true? Without her obedience the Savior would not have been born. Some Christians think that if Mary had refused Gabriel's invitation to bear the Savior, God would have found another woman. There is not the slightest evidence in the New Testament for this view. Mary freely gave herself to God's will of giving the world its Savior. By her instrumentality Mary united the Father to the world through his Son. In a profound sense, Mary united us to the Father through the Son. And that is how we will find a greater degree of unity today. By seeking to imitate her obedience and by seeking submission to the same Father through the Son she bore.

Mary is the spouse of the Holy Spirit. Gabriel proclaimed that the Holy Spirit would come over her and the power of the Most High would overshadow her (Lk 1:35). This is the language of marital love (see Ruth 3:9; Zeph 3:17). Mary was united with the third person of the Trinity in order to give flesh to the second person. As the spouse of the Holy Spirit, she gave her body to the service of God so that she might receive the fullness of God. And so Mary is a sign of how we too must seek to be filled with the Holy Spirit to do the will of God (cf Eph 5:18). It is the Holy Spirit who brings Jesus Christ today just as he brought the divine Christ to the womb of Mary (cf. Jn 14:17,18). When we are filled with the Spirit as Mary was, we are united to Jesus and we become more united with one another. Mary's union with the Holy Spirit brought us the Son who poured out the Spirit that we might be united with both Son and Spirit. Her union brings about our union.

Mary is the mother of the Son. She united his divine and human nature into the one person that would save us from our sins. As Jesus' mother Mary signals that our unity will only be in and through her Son. When Paul says that Jesus was "born of a woman ... that we might receive the adoption." (Gal 4:4,5), the apostle implies that true unity comes only from being members of the same family, in fact the same family in which Jesus is the first-born Son. We cannot be members of many different families that have a tolerance for one another's beliefs and worship. No doubt tolerance for cultural and historical differences is essential, but that is still not the New Testament ideal of unity. Unity means being in the same family as Jesus ("one Lord"), having the same content of belief ("one faith"), living in the same Church body ("one baptism"). Only then can we be sure that we have the same "God and Father of all, who is over all, through all and in all." See Ephesians 4:4-6.

Mary, the Body of Christ and the Eucharist

Real unity requires real communication of Christ's divine nature to God's children. The longer I am a Catholic, the more I understand how necessary was the Incarnation, that supreme act of the eternal Son of God taking human flesh as his own. As the great Church Father Athanasius put it, Christ could not save what he did not assume. If Jesus Christ did not truly take on human nature, he could not save it. Yet God's eternal love for us did just that (Jn 3:16). Nowhere in Scripture is this more pointedly stated than in Hebrews 2:14:

> Since the children have partaken of blood and flesh, he himself [Christ] likewise shared in the same things, so that through his death he might destroy the one who held the power of death, that is, the devil.

Christ's death required a full participation in the human nature we all have. Salvation is the communication, the impartation of that divine person to our human nature. And Mary was the essential instrument of giving our human nature to the divine Son of God. Mary gave what was ours to Jesus that she might give what was his to us. She united our human nature to his divine nature. And because she is the mother of the Church, she now unites his divine person (divine and human) to our humanity so that we might enjoy the fullness of Christ's salvation.

The only way to have real unity among Christians is to have the real Savior unite us. The same body which Mary gave the Son of God must be the instrument of bringing us to the fullness of unity. That is why the Catholic Church has always called the Eucharist the sacrament of unity. It both symbolizes and effects the unity of the Church. This very teaching of the Eucharist as the sacrament of unity should remind every Catholic that unity is not some contrived, negotiated bargain. Unity is the real giving of Christ's life to his mystical body, the Church.

The Catholic Church teaches that the eucharistic bread and wine are the body and blood of Jesus Christ. Taking Jesus' words seriously (one might say literally), the Church holds that the body and blood of Christ are the means of unity among Christians. Paul's words in 1 Co 10:17 are striking, "since there is one bread, we though many are one body for we all partake of the same bread." Paul is teaching an amazing truth. The diverse people in the Church are made one by partaking of the Eucharist. How is this possible? It's not possible if what we eat is simply bread. It's absolutely impossible for a piece of bread to make Christians one in the Church. However, if what we eat is not bread, but the body of Jesus Christ, then Jesus Christ can make us one. We become one body in Christ by taking the one Christ into our bodies (cf. I Co 12:12).

We must understand that the body of Jesus in the Eucharist is not metaphorical, or some additional body to the one he now has in heaven, or that he had on earth. The body of Christ that we receive in the Eucharist is identical with the body he had here on earth and that he has in heaven. And that is why Mary is important. His body was taken from her, not as a generic body but specifically from her body. If Jesus gives us his body in the Eucharist, then Mary is there also giving us her Son in the Eucharist. The body she gave to Jesus is identical with the body that died on the cross and that we receive in the Eucharist.

I realize that for many Christians it will seem dream-like or even absurd to say that the Eucharist gives us the same body as the one that came from Mary. Yet this is the unbroken faith of the early Christian church. Ignatius of Antioch is only one of many witnesses, "They [the heretics] abstain from the Eucharist and prayers in worship because they do not confess that the Eucharist is the body of Jesus Christ our Savior, the same flesh that suffered for our sins and that the Father in kindness raised from the dead." (*Ignatius to the Smyrnaeans* chap 8). Ignatius was a younger contemporary of the last apostle John who died in Ephesus around the early nineties of the first century. This quotation is only one of many such expressions that show how the early Church took Jesus' words seriously, "this is my body." The body of Christ in the Eucharist is *the same body* that hung on the cross and *the same body* that Mary gave to the eternal Son of God. In the previous chapter we saw how the writer of Hebrews emphasized the body of Jesus Christ as our salvation, "Sacrifice and offering You did not desire but a body you have prepared for me." (Heb 10:5); "We have been made holy through the sacrifice of the *body* of Jesus Christ once for all." (Hb 10:10). Jesus' act of hanging on a cross was not optional; he had to suffer if we were to be redeemed. In the same manner, our salvation is conveyed to us through the same body that hung on the cross and is given to us through the Eucharist.

Mary gave us the means to be united in her Son. She gave Jesus his human body and he gave us his body in the institution of the Eucharist. But unity doesn't come about by mechanical reception of the Eucharist. Receiving the body of Christ must be accompanied by the three greatest virtues: faith, hope and love. And Mary can be our best teacher of how to receive Jesus her Son. No one can better show us how to receive properly the Son of God than Mary. She was the one who first received him into the world. She took him into her heart before she had him in her womb. Her words, "let it be done to me according to your word" (Lk 1:38) show how Christ's presence in her life requires dedication of both body and soul. Mary's presence at our communion can also open our hearts to Christ's presence. She reminds us that the full benefit of Christ's indwelling will be ours only if we dedicate our bodies and souls completely to her Son. We are like Mary in this regard. We receive Jesus' body into our bodies and into our souls as well. It is the same body Mary received in seed form that we have in his full humanity. And as the body of the Son of God grew within her, so the same body of Christ must grow within us until the body of the Church reaches the fullness of holiness.

Mary: God's Woman of the Hour

Now is the time for unity among Christians. As we approach the beginning of the third millennium since Christ's birth, we see an almost unprecedented call to unity. Christian leaders the world over have caught a glimpse of Christ's will that "they may be one, Father, as you are in me and I in you." (Jn 17:21). The desire for unity is laudable and ought to be pursued with vigor. Yet the only unity worth pursuing, the only unity that will last is the unity that already exists in the Holy Trinity. This kind of unity is not something we achieve. It is something given to us as a gift. This unity is infused in our souls and expressed by oneness of mind and heart (doctrine & love).

Truth without love is barren and sterile. Unity without truth is empty and fruitless. Jesus was a kind and compassionate man who proclaimed the truth. The Lord who wept over Jerusalem's obstinence (see Mt 23:37-39), and who was moved with compassion over the "sheep without a shepherd" (Mk 6:34) is the same Lord who said that the truth of his words would not pass away (Lk 21:33). If Jesus is our Lord, then we must follow with equal vigor his truth *and* love. Such a commitment implies a rejection of the dilemma I outlined in Chapter Three. Insistence on truth at the expense of unity will not do, nor will embracing unity at the expense of truth. Truth and unity are equally ultimate. Yet even now, we must realize the impossibility of reconciling truth and unity with human schemes and ingenuity. *The only way to have unity is by having unity in Truth.* The truth that brings unity is Jesus himself who is "the way, the truth, and the life." (Jn 14:6). The truth Jesus gives is the complete teaching of his will as expressed in and through the Church of the apostles. The Church is Jesus' idea and institution; it is part of the will of Jesus. And it is Christ's Church that wrote and gave us the Holy Scriptures and the truths of faith passed down from generation to generation. Obedience to Jesus means obedience to Jesus' Church. It is no accident that Christians have spoken of the Church as our mother for centuries. Classic Christianity spoke this way: the one who wants God as a Father must have the Church as a mother. Why is it necessary? Because Jesus is nurturing our faith through our mother, the Church. And that is why Mary is so important.

Jesus is our model, but we must remember that even our Lord learned some of his commitment to truth and compassion from his mother. All we have to assume is that Mary lived her own words to see that this is true. She loved truth enough to consent to Gabriel's invitation to bear the Son of God (Lk 1:38). She was filled with compassion enough to see God's "mercy from generation to generation." (Lk 1:50). Mary was a woman of truth and love. Her commitment to God's truth and love lead her to the unity of the Son of God. Her submissive heart that willingly embraced God's truth and her devoted love for God brought about the unity of Christ's human and divine natures into the perfect unity of his one divine person. So Mary's commitment to truth and unity is both our model and the means of our unity. She modeled our path to unity by her embrace of the divine Son within her womb. We must embrace him too. Mary is also the means of our having unity because without her act of submission to God we would not have the one Savior who can unify us.

It is time to lay down our defensive postures, to lay aside our personal and political agendas, to give up our dearest visions for the church and to embrace the complete will of Christ. I believe that if we could simply be like Mary on that day when Gabriel came to her, we could then say with her, "let it be done to us according to your word." (Lk 1:38). Perhaps, she could say with us:

Lord, we are your servants.
Heal our divisions and
Let Your Son reign as Lord within
Let Your Word dwell within us
And make us one.

Holy Mary, Mother of God, pray for us sinners, now and at the hour of our death.

A FIVE DAY RETREAT WITH JESUS AND MARY

These five days of meditation and reflection are designed to lead the reader into a deeper understanding of and intimacy with Jesus the Lord and Mary his mother. The meditations do not require a lot of theological knowledge, but they do require some degree of openness to growth in faith, hope and love.

Each meditation should take between thirty and sixty minutes and is designed on the model of Ignatius of Loyola's *Spiritual Exercises*. Fruitful spiritual meditation uses the imagination to place oneself back into the biblical story. You should place yourself right there with the characters and experience what they experienced. Each day includes a reading from Scripture, a focal point of meditation that guides you into the story, and a concluding conversation with the biblical personages. Follow this pattern everyday:

1) Begin in the name of the Father, Son and Holy Spirit with a brief prayer that is your own.

2) Read the *focal point* to guide you in reading Scripture.

3) Read the scriptural text fully, slowly, thoughtfully.

4) Read the *Progression of Thought* to help you meditate and visualize the story. Yet don't be afraid to use your imagination and if it leads you in a slightly different direction than what is suggested here, don't be bound by my leading. Let the Spirit

of God lead you, but he will always lead you more deeply into the story. Most of all, don't hurry. Linger with Jesus and Mary for as long as you need and want to. You should not overly worry about whether you are doing the meditation correctly beyond the few guidelines suggested. Let the Spirit of God guide you and trust in Jesus' hold on your life. The goal of the five days is to grow more in love with Jesus and Mary.

5) When you sense a closing of your meditation, have a *Conversation* with Jesus and Mary. Use the suggestions provided, but first and foremost, *ask for the grace to love Jesus better and to love his mother as he does.* Remember that no human creature understands Jesus' heart the way Mary does. Ask our Lord to understand his heart as his mother does.

6) End each day of meditation with this simple prayer: "Jesus, gentle and humble of heart. Make my heart like yours."

DAY ONE

Greeting Jesus and Mary through Gabriel

Scripture Reading: Luke 1:26-38

Focal Point: We receive with joy Gabriel's message that a Savior will redeem us and contemplate Mary as God's chosen instrument of salvation.

Progression of Thought: As you sit next to Mary, you hear the rushing sound of an angel from heaven. Mary and you are startled. But you are even more amazed when you hear Gabriel say, "Hail, full of grace one." Why did you give Mary so exalted a title, Gabriel? What could this possibly mean? Angel of God, has any other woman ever be given this title?

Mary, I understand your fear, your bewilderment. You're not yet married. The embarrassment and scorn waiting for you will be enormous. Yet the angel's words are so full of hope: "The Son of the most High," "the throne of his Father David," "a kingdom without end."

It does sound impossible, doesn't it? But "with God nothing will be impossible." Somehow I see that you know this Mary. God is the God of miracles. What's that you said? You, the handmaiden of the Lord? Gabriel just said you were full of grace. I sense a deep mystery. You are exalted, Mary. Yet your humility is so evident. What is humility, Mary? Is it submitting to God's holy will? Is it bearing God in our bodies?

Conversation: Talk with Jesus and ask him to help you love his mother the way he does. If you can, ask Mary to help you love Jesus for no human being has ever loved him as much as his mother. Ask that you might know the joy of Mary's humility and her expectation of the birth of the Savior.

DAY TWO

With Elizabeth: Greeting Mary and Jesus

Scripture Reading: Luke 1:39-56

Focal Point: We greet the Savior with Elizabeth's humility by using her own words, "how is it that the mother of my Lord would come to me?"

Progression of Thought: You sit in the corner of a small house while silently you watch Elizabeth clean. She goes about her daily responsibilities with an unprecedented joy. In her old age, Elizabeth knows she will have a son. Who would have dreamed it? You smile as you see the joy on her face.

Suddenly, the door opens. Mary, what are you doing here? No sooner does Mary speak than Elizabeth feels her stomach move. The old woman's face changes into a sweet smile that reflects a new inner peace. It is as if God has come to Elizabeth's heart. The evidence of the Spirit's work is here. Elizabeth cannot contain herself. "Blessed are you among women and blessed is the fruit of your womb." Can I say those words about Mary? The fruit of Mary's womb is certainly blessed. The fruit is the Son of God. But what about Mary herself? Of course, Elizabeth is right! How could any woman not be blessed if she carried within her God himself? Can it really be that God was in Mary's womb? Isn't that an exaggeration? Yet, what else could the words mean, "how is it that the mother of my Lord would come to me?"

Sit down, Mary. Let me think about you and the divine One in your womb. Is what Elizabeth says true? "Blessed is she who believed that there would be a fulfillment of those things spoken by the Lord." This seems to be the key to understanding your life — faith. Your faith and mine.

I can see that Mary is about to burst with joy. She can't hold back her joy. She must sing. Sit and listen to Mary's song of joy.

Conversation: Ask Jesus for the grace to live by faith as Mary. Ask to believe as she did. Seek the joy of knowing God's presence through Mary's presence just as Mary brought God's presence to Elizabeth. If you are able, talk with Mary about coming to know her Son as she did. Jesus is waiting to reveal himself to you and to show how much he respects and loves his mother. Ask him for that gift of faith. Jesus will help you see Mary as Elizabeth did, a faith-filled woman who was blessed above all women.

DAY THREE

A Savior is Born to Us

Scripture Reading: Luke 2:1-20

Focal Point: Like the poor shepherds, we go to Bethlehem to find the infant King and his family. Like Mary, we contemplate the mystery of her Son's incarnation.

Progression of Thought: It is a quiet night in the Judean hills. We sit by the campfire with the sheep under control. Where is that light coming from? From that angel! How can we get away from its blinding force? Then again. Why do we want to? Great joy, you say? The birth of every child is great joy. What's so special about this birth? Israel's Savior? A descendant of David? Where is such a child? How will we find him, and having found him, recognize him? Lying in a manger? A cattle stall is a rather simple, even crude place to put the Messiah, the Savior of the world. This contrast is striking. Heavenly messengers heralding such a simple birth. Yet what else could aptly proclaim the world-wide impact of Christ's salvation?

Bethlehem. Are you Joseph and Mary from Nazareth? An angel told us of your coming. Has the baby been born yet? Yes? May we see him? Oh, yes. There he is in the manger. It is just as the angel told us. Everything has been fulfilled just like we were told. Can we tell you what the angel told us?

Mary seems especially quiet and subdued. Others are shouting praise to God, but she sits in a spirit of contemplation. What are you turning over in your mind, Mary? Do you know or see something here that we don't see? Do you have some special insight into your Son's birth?

Conversation: Ask Jesus to show you how his birth signaled his world-wide kingdom by joining together heaven and earth. Ask him how you can be a part of his kingdom? Ask Mary to teach you how to contemplate the mystery of her Son's birth? Maybe we become members of his kingdom by doing what Mary did i.e. guard these things in our hearts and turn them over in our minds (Lk 2:19).

DAY FOUR

The Infant King and His Mother

Scripture Reading: Matthew 2:1-12

Focal Point: We must worship Christ with the gift of our lives and honor his mother who is always with him.

Progression of Thought: It has been such a long journey. Finally, we're in Jerusalem. Herod the king will surely know where this royal infant is to be born. King Herod seems disturbed, doesn't he? Wouldn't you be if a new king were born? Wouldn't you be worried for the future of your own reign? The wise men search the Scriptures for the Messiah's birth. Bethlehem in Judah. Yes, of course. This is what the prophet Micah foretold.

As we walk the streets of Jerusalem, we sense the disapproval of its residents. Yet, I don't understand. The Jewish Scriptures predict the coming of Gentile kings when the Messiah is born. Why would Jerusalem be so disturbed at our arrival? At least we have Herod's approval to search diligently for the child. Yet, I wonder. Is Herod really sincere in his desire to see the child? Anyone can see that a new king would be a threat to his throne.

Do you see the star moving again? Let's go. It's moving toward Bethlehem. What joy fills our hearts as we "see the child with Mary his mother." We recognize immediately that this is the child we have been searching for and the one we should worship. We must give him the best of our wealth. Gold, frankincense and myrrh. The complete gift of ourselves.

Conversation: Imagine Jesus as a child. You worship him by opening the gift of your heart to him. You recognize him as God. He alone is God, but he is never alone. Mary is there with him and with you. Ask Mary to show you how to love Jesus. She points to him as she did at the wedding feast of Cana. Love is a never ending journey. Mary is there to help you peal back the layers of self which keep you from loving Jesus "with all your soul, heart and strength."

DAY FIVE

With Mary, Jesus and the Beloved Disciple at the Cross

Scripture Reading: John 19: 23-27

Focal Point: To place ourselves in the position of the beloved disciple and to hear Jesus' words to us about our relationship to Mary.

Progression of Thought: The cross is awful. The sight is hideous. Human beings crucified are treated as vermin. And my Master is the Son of God. How could even the most vile human powers condone and perform such an evil deed? Are these soldiers so callous that they care nothing for my Master's pain? What can I do? Maybe only to "stand by the cross of Jesus."

Even now, at the bitter end of his life, I look into my Master's eyes and I feel the love he has for me. I feel like a beloved disciple. If he loves me, how much more must he love his mother? What's that? He's trying to say something. "Woman, behold your son." Me? Mary's son? Oh, Master. That seems almost cruel. You are her Son. Surely, no one can take your place. What could these words possibly mean? Mary, will you continue your maternal care over me?

He's ready to speak again. Jesus, what do you want to say? I know it must be painful even to speak? "Behold, your mother." Mary, my mother? That seems a gift too great for someone like me to receive. Yet, in your eyes, dear Jesus. I see your thoughts. "Yes, you are unworthy my beloved disciple. But I love you enough to give you my mother as your mother. Take her as your own." Now I see Jesus' love shining through this dark hour. His love is fulfilled in her love for me.

Conversation: Your conversational prayer now takes place at the foot of the cross. Thank Jesus for the infinite gift of his life. Accept him once more as your Lord and Savior. Accept the cross he gives you. Most of all, accept the mother he gives you. Have you received Jesus as your personal Lord? Have you received Mary as your personal mother? Ask both Jesus and Mary to give you a heart united to their hearts.

FOR FURTHER READING

Books on the Mother of Jesus are legion, and so I have made the following suggestions for those readers who are unfamiliar with books about Mary, and yet who wish to explore this topic more. Those mentioned here are recommended primarily because they are balanced treatments of Scripture and Catholic doctrine. There is no better place to begin than Dr. Mark Miravalle's *Introduction to Mary The Heart of Marian Doctrine and Devotion* (Santa Barbara: Queenship Publishing Company, 1993). Mark Miravalle treats Scripture, Church documents and the history of devotion to Mary in short compass. Many of the topics that I only touch on in this book are developed more fully there. Chapter Seven gives brief answers to traditional objections about Marian dogmas for those who need to resolve those kind of questions.

Many meditative studies on Mary's life have been written, but one that leads the reader into deeper understanding of Mary in Scripture is Frederico Suarez's *Mary of Nazareth* (New York: Scepter Press, 1985 3rd printing). A fuller and more scholarly treatment of Mary in Scripture can be found in Stefano Manelli's *All Generations Shall Call Me Blessed: Biblical Mariology* (New Bedford, MA, 1995). As a reference tool, Michael O'Carroll's *Theotokos: A Theological Encyclopedia of the Blessed Virgin Mary* (Collegeville, MN: The Liturgical Press, 1982) is indispensable for in-depth study of Mary.

The most important prayer involving Mary is the Rosary. One of the best modern guides is Romano Guardini's *The Rosary of Our*

Lady (Manchester, NH: Sophia Institute Press, 1994). Guardini was a prominent theologian in Germany who had a profound devotion to Jesus' mother. His book will lead any Christian to a deeper prayer life by properly using the Rosary.

Many Christians, both Catholic and non-Catholic, are confused by reported Marian apparitions and private revelations. Some of the books on these phenomena are of questionable value, and so the reader must be discerning. No better guide for understanding what the Catholic Church teaches about apparitions and revelations can be found than Benedict Groeschel's *A Still Small Voice: A Practical Guide to Reported Revelations* (San Francisco: Ignatius Press, 1993). This book is one of the most balanced treatments available in explaining how the Church arrives at its judgments in these matters.

About the Author

Kenneth J. Howell is Associate Director of the *Coming Home Network International.* A Presbyterian minister from 1978 to 1996, Dr. Howell converted to the Catholic Church in June of 1996. Dr. Howell holds a Master of Divinity degree from Westminster Theological Seminary in Philadelphia, Penn. and a Ph.D. in General Linguistics from Indiana. He also holds a Ph.D. from Lancaster University (U.K.) in History.

Dr. Howell's journey to the Catholic Church began in an intense way while he was Associate Professor of Biblical Languages and Literature at Reformed Theological Seminary in Jackson, Mississippi, a position he held for seven years. His own teaching of Sacred Scripture and the Church Fathers led Dr. Howell to the Catholic belief in the reality of Christ's body in the Eucharist. This journey ended his twenty year search for the true Church of Jesus Christ that found its fulfillment in coming home to the fullness of the Catholic faith.

Dr. Howell is married to the former Sharon Canfield and has three teenage children. He may be contacted at:

814 Eddington Court
Bloomington, Indiana 47401
(812) 339-4139
khowell@indiana.edu